Lost in the SYSTEM

Charlotte Lopez

WITH SUSAN DWORKIN

A FIRESIDE BOOK   Published by Simon & Schuster

FIRESIDE
Rockefeller Center
1230 Avenue of the Americas
New York, NY 10020

FIRESIDE and colophon are registered trademarks
of Simon & Schuster Inc.

Designed by Bonni Leon-Berman

Manufactured in the United States of America

1   3   5   7   9   10   8   6   4   2

Library of Congress Cataloging-in-Publication Data
Lopez, Charlotte, date.
Lost in the system / Charlotte Lopez ; with Susan Dworkin.
p.   cm.
"A Fireside book."
1. Lopez, Charlotte, 1976–   .   2. Foster children—Vermont—
Biography.   3. Foster home care—Vermont.
4. Beauty contestants—Vermont—Biography.
I. Dworkin, Susan.   II. Title.
HV883.V5L66   1996
362.7′33′092—dc20
[B]   96-2374
CIP
ISBN 0-684-81199-5

*This book is dedicated
to all the kids in this country
who are still lost in the system.*

OREWORD

MY BIG SISTER, Charlotte, has never been able to keep her mouth shut.

Whatever issue is on the table, she's got to chew it over, spit it out, discuss it and analyze it, argue all the sides, and tell it exactly like it is.

Other people try to keep their emotions under control so they can think. Charlotte tries to set her emotions free so she can *feel*.

When I read this book, it took me back to our babyhood and our childhood, and it reminded me of our wonderful sisterhood, which has never failed us, never.

So if you want to know the truth about the true thoughts and feelings of one of those 450,000 or so foster kids who live like a big sleeping secret in our country, then listen to my sister the beauty queen, the national advocate for foster kids.

She's been there. I've been there. And it hasn't always been easy, but we're doing fine.

We are the lucky ones.

Diana Wensley

$\mathscr{A}$UTHOR'S NOTE

I HAVE CHANGED the names and otherwise disguised many of the people in this book in order to protect their privacy. This holds true, for example, for the kids I lived with in the group foster home. Those who appear as themselves are the people who agreed to be interviewed or gave express permission to be identified. The only exceptions to that are some individuals whose names and faces have already appeared in national media —for example, my mother, my former foster parents, and some of my wonderful friends from the Miss Teen USA Pageant.

Unfortunately, Bill and Cari Wensley chose to decline offers to be interviewed for this book. I have tried to be mindful of their point of view throughout, however. Obviously, we had our differences. But I will always be grateful for their care and concern and for all they did to help me reach this point in my life.

Special thanks are due to those who agreed to be interviewed and helped me flesh out my own understanding of my experience as a foster child, most especially William M. Young, commissioner of Social and Rehabilitation Services of Vermont. I also wish to thank Susan Dworkin and our editor Cindy Gitter for their help with this manuscript. I am grateful to my parents Jill and Al, to Janet Henry, to my wonderful sister Diana and my brother Duane, and above all to the good Lord, whose guidance allowed me to be confident in knowing there is nothing that cannot be achieved when you have faith in yourself.

Lost in the SYSTEM

$\mathcal{I}$NTRODUCTION

I BELIEVE IN fate.

I honestly, truly believe that fate sets aside a certain amount of good fortune for each and every one of us.

The trick is to notice it.

I mean, opportunity doesn't generally come on like Queen Latifah. Most likely it sort of tickles you and whispers: *Wake up, kid, this is your big chance.* And if you're too tired out or bummed with a bad, blue altitude—or just unlucky—you could miss it entirely.

I was lucky.

I grew up in foster care in Vermont. In and out of homes until I was three, then a placement with one family until I was a freshman in high school, then several years in a group foster care home, where I lived with a bunch of tough, funny, troubled, street-smart kids.

In all those years, I had never been adopted.

One sunny Sunday morning in that group foster care home, I was just hanging out, sort of browsing through the paper, dreaming about escaping from my little life, longing desperately to have a home and a family of my own, when I just happened to notice this ad for the Miss Vermont Teen USA Pageant. "Come and try out," it said. "You can be on national television with Dick Clark." There was an 800 number you could call.

I felt this tremendous rush of excitement, because I had been watching the pageant for years on television.

Maybe because I had been flipped around from one foster home to another when I was little, maybe because I never really felt secure, maybe because I felt so completely helpless to control anything that happened to me in the foster care system, I always loved the big talent shows, like *Star Search* and Miss Universe, where nobodies became somebodies, and people who weren't famous went out and did the best they could and transformed their lives. When we were girls together growing up, my sister Diana and I had watched all the pageants, every year, without fail. We even kept score. We enjoyed seeing the girls from all over out there modeling and entertaining. We'd imagine being on stage and imitate the way they walked down the runways in that certain special primping, mincing way, and we'd grin and take pictures and proclaim our victory speeches to the meadows and the mountains of Vermont.

It wasn't that I thought I would grow up and be a beauty queen. It was the entertainment part, the being-appreciated-and-applauded part that got to me: the attention that I had always missed, that I seemed always to want more of.

And here it was, in the Bennington newspaper—a window into the house of dreams.

From this ad, I would soon find my way into the Miss Vermont Teen USA contest . . . and as fate would have it, I would win. From there, I would go to the national finals in Biloxi, Mississippi. I would walk down a *real* runway, wear a *real* evening gown. The cheers and applause I'd always desired would resound through the hall as I became Miss Teen USA 1993, with a crown and a huge bouquet of roses and fabulous prizes. Because of that experience, I am a college student today —something I dreamed of but never dared to expect. Because of that experience, I have had a chance to meet foster kids from all over, to hear what they have to say, and to be a national spokesperson for the almost half a million American kids who are in foster care at any given moment in our country.

How strange fate is! How crazy and surprising are the tides of fortune!

CHAPTER ONE

My Mother's Name Is Emma

MY MOTHER'S NAME is Emma. She is mentally unbalanced. Upon occasion, she has been a homeless bag lady. I've heard stories that she lived in the house at the cemetery where they keep the bodies during the frozen snowy Vermont winters when it's too cold to bury the dead. I've seen letters that she wrote to our social workers, after they took us away from her and placed us in foster care. She begs to see us. She promises to be good and take care of us. But she couldn't take care of us, because she was mentally unbalanced.

I found Emma when I was seventeen, not in the flesh but in my case files at SRS (Social and Rehabilitation Services) in Vermont. Before these incredible documents were sealed forever, I finally got to read them. It's a fantastic experience, like watching yourself in a movie that was made when you had no idea the camera was running.

Imagine a set of files three or four inches thick, covering every aspect of your life from the time that you were a tiny little kid, in which social workers recorded every visit they had, every phone call they made or received from people connected to you, every diagnosis from every doctor, every complaint about your behavior, every grade you made in school. What a trip! Of course, the entries generally record what people said *about* me, but not what I might have said about myself. Me, I rarely spoke to my social workers before I was a teenager, and by that time I had learned to say mostly what I thought would please or mollify them.

From these files, I learned that Emma was born in Puerto Rico, lived in the Bronx until she was in the tenth grade, went back to Puerto Rico, finished high school, did two years in college as a business major, and worked in public relations for three years. Then she returned to New York, got a clerical job, and in 1967 married a guy named Manuel Caraballo. They had at least one baby: my brother, Duane, now a musician in Colorado.

Emma left her husband in 1968. She couldn't hold a job and ended up on welfare. She told a social worker that the reason for her instability was that some Colombian people she boarded with were trying to control her mind through hypnotic powers. These mysterious forces that Emma believed to be invading her life were so powerful, she said, that they sent demons to rape her while she slept—on Christmas Eve in 1975, when I was conceived, and on Christmas Eve in 1976, when my sister Diana was conceived.

After I was born—in Puerto Rico on September 25, 1976—Emma put Duane and me into a foster home. It would be the first of several. I was a little baby, and I suppose I don't remember. But the psychologists say that you really do remember, deep in your subconscious—you remember being in somebody's arms and feeling bonded, and then being put into another set of arms and having to learn to feel bonded again.

When you're that young, it isn't a problem. As long as it doesn't happen repeatedly.

But it did.

Demons in Vermont

EMMA LEFT PUERTO Rico in 1977 and headed directly for Vermont, which she had decided was the best place in which to raise her children and "escape" from her Colombian "demons." Maybe she figured that being from a warm southern climate, they would not want to follow her to a place dominated by snow, ice, dense fog, and towering mountains.

When SRS found her, she was literally nine months pregnant and had no place to live and no way to take care of Duane and me. They took her to Putnam Hospital on September 29 to have Diana, and she signed an agreement to put me and Duane into a temporary foster home (my second). Eventually, SRS reunited us with our mother and new baby sister and settled us in an apartment in Manchester.

Manchester is a tiny little town where everybody pretty much sees what's going on in everybody else's life. Nosiness. Gossip. It's the worst thing about living in a state with only a little more than half a million people—and the best thing, too, in my case, because the snoopy neighbors, witnessing Emma's neglect, began watching over us, bringing us in from the cold, and reporting to SRS that we were in big trouble. The truth is, I think nosiness and gossip saved our lives.

Duane was bilingual, speaking Spanish and English both. Maybe because he had been a baby in happier times—when Emma wasn't so deranged—he spoke her language and could communicate with her. He somehow also managed to go to school and care for her, and he really tried to take care of us, too. But he was just a little boy! How much could he do? She'd scream at him and hit him, and he'd run away. She'd lock him in the house and he'd break a window to escape. When the landlord locked Emma out for not paying her rent, she broke a window to climb back in. We stayed on in the apartment, without heat, electricity, hot water, or furniture.

One of the neighbors gave Emma chairs, tables, towels, dishes. SRS would give her money for food, but she'd go over to the market, lose track of who she was and where she was, and forget to buy anything. So we'd go hungry. Folks in Manchester remember her stomping up and down on the porch, drunk and raving, having shouting matches with people who weren't there. She was picked up for soliciting in the streets. When Emma wandered off, she would leave Diana and me to lie around in our filthy diapers.

Because we had no good food to eat, we suffered from all kinds of nutritional deficiency disorders. My hair was falling out. Because we had nothing to play with and no place to run to, our bones and muscles didn't grow. I couldn't see well; Diana couldn't hear well. We were so neglected and isolated that we weren't learning to talk right. Emotionally and physically, we were vegetables.

The neighbors would complain, and the cops would come and find us playing in the garbage, take us away for a bit, and then bring us back to Emma. The school would call to say Duane hadn't been attending, and Emma would declare that her "voices" had forbidden her to send him. One nice gentleman saw me playing in the driveway in my underwear on a winter day. He came out and wrapped me in a coat, then took me into his store and demanded that the authorities do something to rescue us. (Years later, when I won the Miss Teen USA Pageant, I was visiting Manchester and noticed that a man across the street was staring at me. He was our old neighbor, still minding the same store. He couldn't believe that the abused little girl whose crazy mother used to let her run outside in the snow in her underwear had become Miss Teen USA.)

A kindly social worker tried to explain to Emma that she was in danger of losing us. Because he had an Italian surname, she decided he was a Mafia criminal who had been sent by the demon powers to torment her. Finally, when she became violent and threatened the other tenants in her building, the authorities arrested her and the kindly social worker got a temporary order to have us sent to live with a nice family—the Taylors.

I was two years old.

Escape, Part 1

THE TAYLORS WERE affectionate people, with a pleasant house and a bunch of kids. But they scared me to death. The idea of being with strange people and going to sleep in a strange room just terrified me. They had to take me for all kinds of therapy, because between the neglect, the filth, the bad nutrition, and the prolonged periods of silence and darkness in Emma's house, I was intellectually and physically way below normal for my age.

Diana was in terrible shape, too. But because she was one year younger, she was much more relaxed with the Taylors than I was. It took her about a day and a half to get used to them; it took me maybe a week or two.

Once the Taylor home become comfortable for me, I wanted to stay there forever. I desperately wanted a family; that's human instinct. I didn't make a judgment as to which family was best for me. If there was a mommy and maybe a daddy and a home and a bed and food on the table and a loving mood and warmth and *peace,* I was just fine.

But then, because our social workers were part of a system that believed their responsibility was to keep us in contact with our *natural* mother, they would take us out of this place where we were trying to learn to love the people in order to arrange a visit with Emma. On those occasions, I would throw a hysterical fit—screaming, crying, running all over the house, trying to hide. As the hour of our departure approached, I'd cower off by myself. Throughout the trip, I'd stand in the back of the social worker's car, staring out the window, mumbling, "Don't leave me, don't leave me."

Deep down in my toddler brain, I must have had some inkling of just how eager Emma really was to see me. Said one of the social workers: "When we brought the girls to Mrs. Caraballo, it was almost as if we were delivering the groceries." It was clear that she was incompetent as a parent and that we'd be in real danger if we returned to her. It was also perfectly clear that she really didn't care that much whether we were with her or not—out of twelve possible visits she could have had with us while we were with the Taylors, Emma managed to make only three. But when the day of our custody hearing arrived, Emma fought like a tiger to keep us. Unluckily for us, the state of Vermont provided her with a really crackerjack lawyer, who argued that our detention in foster care was no good because "a finding of fact had never been formally heard" and because we had been held in detention by SRS "in excess of the prescribed time for such detention." What that meant, in plain English, was that we hadn't been taken away from her in quite the right way, so we had to be returned. In a couple of hours, the whole case that SRS had laboriously made to rescue us from Emma's tender mercies had been thrown out on a technicality.

FOUR DAYS AFTER she got us back, Emma was spotted wandering drunk around the neighborhood. Her lawyer had promised that she would continue to take us for visits to doctors and speech therapists that the Taylors had begun. We never got there. We were left alone again, malnourished again, filthy again. The electricity was turned off because Emma didn't pay her bills. She used candles to light the house and cooked over an open flame. Our apartment rapidly became one of the leading firetraps in southern Vermont.

Emma said that the "demonic hypnotist" who "controlled" her mind was forcing her not to do the things her lawyer had promised she would do. She also said that it was Duane's fault —that he was supposed to watch his little sisters and he hadn't done his job. And anyway, she said, Diana and I didn't need medical attention or speech therapy. That was just something SRS was inventing to make her life difficult.

Finally our brother Duane solved the situation—by the only means available to most kids who need to change their lives. He got into trouble. All of a sudden, a kid who had never done anything wrong started turning up with things he just happened to "find"—like somebody's bike.

If it was a gambit, it sure worked.

The cops had always felt intimidated by the law that favors the natural parents and were reluctant to be a part of any effort to take us away from Emma. As long as Duane was a good boy, there was no real way to show that her behavior was hurting him, so there was no real reason to pull him out of there. But now that Duane was beginning to act out, the cops could easily conclude that "without adequate adult supervision, it was only a matter of time before Duane got into more serious trouble."

The petty thievery did it. The authorities were finally *noticing* Duane, and by extension, his little sisters. On September 12, 1979, after six long, scary months with Emma, we were sent back to the Taylors. It was great. Emma just let her visitation appointments go by. We saw her less and less.

Every once in a while, without warning, she would call and

say, "I'm coming over." We'd hang out all day with the social worker, waiting for Emma to show. And then, of course, she wouldn't.

Somewhere in there, I stopped waiting for her. Somewhere in there, SRS decided that they had better start looking toward "the eventual termination of parental rights." Why had it taken SRS so long to decide to go for it and take us away from Emma? Bill Young, who has been Commissioner of the Department of Social and Rehabilitation Services in Vermont since 1985, explained: "The public doesn't really understand how traumatic it is for kids to be separated from their parents, even in the most horrendous situations. So child welfare systems throughout the country have the presumption that kids are better off with their parents. *If you are going to break that tie, you'd better be absolutely sure that it has to break.*"

Our good luck was that Emma left Vermont. She promised to return with enough resources to make a home for herself and all three of us. But that never happened. Our *bad* luck was that the Taylors decided to get a divorce. Mrs. Taylor moved out with her daughters. Our brother Duane stayed with Mr. Taylor and his son. Diana and I were placed with another family—the Petersons. It was my fourth foster care placement. We stayed with the Petersons for the better part of four months. Not a very long time, really—but long enough to give this girl a permanent lifelong case of the dislocation blues.

Escape, Part 2

THE PETERSONS LIVED in a trailer.

I thought it was heavenly.

They gave us a really nice room. It was a bright, sunshiny

yellow, with two windows. Our bedspreads were yellow. It made everything cheery. Mrs. Peterson's mother (we called her Grammy) remembers that we arrived with one tiny little bag between us, containing a couple of pairs of socks and some underwear—and not one toy. If Mrs. Peterson threw away a piece of leftover bread or some uneaten macaroni, I would scream and cry and make her take it out of the garbage and wrap it up and put it away. You see, to the chronically underfed, every crust is precious.

Grammy was sweet and chubby and soft and full of smiles. She always bought things for us. We soon had a plastic Fisher-Price stove and a little shopping cart.

I felt that Mrs. Peterson really liked both of us and that she really liked me. But I was totally sure that Mr. Peterson never liked me at all, even though he seemed to love Diana.

Once we were out playing ball, and he looked out the window. Diana waved, and he waved back. I waved, and he shut the window. I remember the horrible pain I got in my stomach, the sadness and frustration. I was desperate for love. I tried so hard to be as good and lovable as possible. But he just didn't like me. I pretended I didn't notice (I learned to do that a lot) and continued to play ball. These repressed feelings have affected me to this day. Am I making this up? I don't think so. People *do* have favorites. They always pick and choose the kids they prefer —in school, at home. So why not Mr. Peterson?

One time—oh, I'll never forget this—I had on training pants (white with blue flowers), and by accident I went to the bathroom in them. I was so embarrassed. Mr. Peterson got really mad at me and humiliated me even more by forcing me to clean out my underwear. I stood on a chair, washing my pants in the sink. Mrs. Peterson was helping me. I was crying. Meanwhile, Mr. Peterson was holding Diana on his lap, reading her a book.

I was three years old. I remember wanting him to accept me and wondering why he wouldn't. I hadn't done anything for him not to like me. I couldn't stand it!

In June, the Petersons told our social worker that we would have to go. Not that we were bad—just that they were having family squabbles, and Mrs. Peterson was pregnant, and there was too much stress. Grammy tried really hard to get SRS to let us come and live with her. She was divorced, and she had a big house and a good job and really loved us and would have gladly adopted us. But the adoption rules in those days favored *married* people. Our social workers were bound and determined to put us with a solid Mom-and-Dad family. I was really sad at having to leave Grammy. Even though I was only a little kid and I had known her only a couple of months, I never forgot her because she had offered us so much love and kindness.

One day our social worker came over. He was a really fun guy. I liked him because because he was always nice to me. He put us in his car and took us for a visit with some people called the Wensleys, who lived in Shaftsbury. I remember the ride because it was a sweltering day in July, the car was really hot, and I burned my thighs on the seat.

When it turned out that we were getting ready to *stay* at the Wensleys—that we would soon be leaving the Petersons, the sunny yellow room and the tiny kitchen in the trailer and Mrs. Peterson and Grammy—I figured it was my fault. I figured it was because I was a bad little girl and people didn't like me.

Moving In with Bill and Cari

MY FIRST VISIT to Bill and Cari Wensley's house is still vivid in my mind.

I remember walking up the front steps. Diana followed me

(she followed me everywhere). It was a small colonial-style house, with only two bedrooms. But to my mind, it seemed HUGE! I had never been in a house with stairs, and I was totally awed by that. Cari Wensley was pretty. She had beautiful long brown hair, which I admired very much because I had a thing about hair, since mine was so patchy and ugly, always falling out. Bill had red hair and a mustache, and he was kind of wiry and slender. They had an adorable baby named Billy.

When we arrived, it seemed to me that Billy got all the attention and not me. That was a big thing with me, not having attention. It made me nervous and frightened, and a little angry. They offered us iced tea in these neat green plastic cups, with tops. I didn't want the top on my cup. I thought I was too big for one.

Cari said, "If you're not going to drink it with a top, you're not going to have it at all."

I replied, "Fine! Who cares? I don't want it anyway!"

Diana stayed right behind me, every minute. If I said, "I have to go up the stairs," she said, "Me, too." If I said, "I want to go outside," she said, "Me, too." I guess I was like her mother in a way, because I was the only person who had always been there for her, from the beginning, every day, without interruptions or separations. Each of us had become an anchor for the other. So whatever I did, she did. And wherever I went, I expected her to follow.

I said, "I'm going to the bathroom."

Diana repeated, "Me, too."

Cari said she would take us.

I said, "No."

Diana repeated, "No."

So the social worker took us to the bathroom.

In his report, he called our behavior "initial testing"—that's social work-ese for when kids feel out a new situation by trying to see what will happen if they are "bad." He concluded that the

Wensleys seemed to understand and that the visit went pretty well. And about a week later, the deal was done. We moved in with Cari and Bill Wensley in Shaftsbury, Vermont. It was my fifth foster care placement. I was almost four years old.

CARI TOLD OUR social worker that when we first arrived, I would say "I love you" twenty times a day. Then I totally stopped—and I couldn't get those words past my lips again until maybe a year later. I was always asking if I could be Cari's child, always begging for reassurance.

> *When will you adopt me?*
> *Do you like me as much as you like Billy?*
> *Do you like me as much as you like Diana?*
> *Can I pretend I came out of your tummy?*
> *Are you going to let Emma come and take me away?*
> *Are you going to adopt me?*

I was afraid of everything and mad at everybody, even the people who were helping me, like my social workers and foster parents. I was mad at the Taylors for letting me go, mad at the Petersons for letting me go, mad at little Billy because he was so cute and at Diana because she was always underfoot. Of course, if she hadn't been, I would have been mad at that too.

I didn't trust anyone. How could I have? I had been constantly moved in and out of these homes and never educated about the situation I was in. So I thought it was my fault—that I was being rejected and forced to move because I had some kind of disease or I had done something wrong. By the time I moved in with the Wensleys, I had given up. Four years old and already feeling like a failure!

My conversations with myself went like this:

Who needs this? They're not going to love me. Why should I bother liking them? I don't even care if they love me anyway. They're going to feed me? Fine. I like being fed. They're going to give me a bed? Great. Because I need a bed to sleep in. But that's it! I'm not going to let myself get my hopes up again.

"When they came to us, the girls were in pretty rough shape," Bill Wensley would later tell *Glamour* magazine.

"For several years they had terrible nightmares," Cari added. "There were nights when I would get up eight times."

If something upset me, I would scream and pout and mumble and whine under my breath—a kind of demented behavior I may have learned from observing Emma. I was also obsessed with spiders, wolves, witches, snakes, probably because of Emma's babblings about demonic forces. Even fairy tales were a danger zone. Cari would try to read us stories every night before bed. If the story had a witch in it like "Hansel and Gretel," or a wicked stepmother like "Cinderella," or dwarfs like "Snow White," I would howl and go limp in protest.

I also had a very peculiar way of expressing myself. Instead of saying "May I go outside?" I would say "I can't go outside," as though I anticipated that I wouldn't be allowed to go outside, because of all the times Emma had said "You can't."

Physically we were both pathetic. Diana's limbs were skinny, her stomach distended. And I was terribly weak, because I hadn't had any exercise during my crucial toddler years, and the big muscles in my legs and back just hadn't developed. I couldn't run properly, and I fell down a lot. Cari and Bill bought us ladders so we would climb and grow strong. They bought me a tricycle.

Strange dogs scared us. If Cari let Diana and me into the yard to play, we would take a stick with us to hit any neighborhood dog on the tail and shoo it away. And planes terrified us. If we heard one overhead, we would run for the house and pound on the door, shouting for help.

I remember hiding.

They were looking for me and I was hiding in the Tupperware cabinet. I threw the Tupperware out and got in and closed the door. When they found me, I made a gruesome face, for which I became famous in my foster family.

The Wensleys reported to our social worker one day that I came home from nursery school and told Bill, "I don't want to live here anymore."

"Why?" he asked. "Is it because we spank you when you're naughty?"

"No," I said. "But I've lived here a long time. And now it's time to go."

Once again, Diana adjusted much more quickly than I did. Cari told a visitor that Diana was easy—that she would do anything she was asked to do—but that I was troublesome, disobedient, rebellious. The year's difference in our ages apparently made all the difference, freeing Diana's subconscious from some of the lousier baby memories that haunted me. She just adapted more easily. She didn't feel as terrified of relocation and rejection.

The truth is, she never has.

The Wonderful Treasure Wars

INITIALLY DIANA SLEPT in a crib and I slept in a bed, but we cried and cried all night and drove everybody else in the house crazy, so they put us together in a double bed, where we cuddled up next to each other and slept more soundly. SRS had a rule that each foster child had to have a separate bed, but clearly an exception had to be made here. We were just too insecure to sleep separately.

When we calmed down a little, Cari and Bill got us bunk beds. We were so excited with them! They were like a live-in play palace to us! I would tuck blankets under the top mattress so they would hang down and close in the whole bottom part. That meant we could pretend we had a house with an upstairs and a downstairs. At first, when we were shy and frightened, we just got all snuggledy in there and played quietly. But when we grew more confident and secure, we suddenly discovered a wealth of youthful energy, and we'd transform the beds into forts and play "War!" I'd take my stuffed animals in with me to be my soldiers in the bottom fort. My Care Bear would be the Commanding General. Our everyday weapons were rubber bands. But the rubber bands with plastic balls that Cari put in our hair were the heavy artillery.

After a while, Billy got old enough to join us and play "Capture the Treasure." We had little banks from Kmart that we called our Treasure Boxes. We would all hide our Treasure Boxes somewhere on our half of the bunk bed. Then the other players would try to capture the others' Treasure Boxes and the priceless collection of bobby pins and Lego sections and wooden beads and pennies and pretty colored pebbles inside, and the battle would rage in a hail of giggles and rubber bands.

It was so much fun! It was the beginning of real fun for me, and I loved it! *I loved enjoying myself.* Most kids just enjoy themselves automatically; they're not afraid because they've never been afraid, and they don't even notice that they're laughing. But me, I really knew that this was a better life than the one I had had, that there was nothing automatic about having the chance to laugh and play.

Family Values

HOLIDAYS WERE ALWAYS big events at the Wensleys. I don't recall celebrating them before we moved there. We would always be excited at least a couple of weeks before the actual holiday, because of how much the family hyped them. During Halloween, Cari always helped us get our costumes together. We were not allowed to be anything evil or satanic, so I was Little Bo Peep one year, then a gypsy, a mom, a bag lady. Bill would take the green trailer we used to lug our garbage to the dump and fill it with hay, so that we could all sit in it while he pulled us around the neighborhood to trick or treat. At Thanksgiving we would always have lots of relatives over, and Cari and all the aunts and grandmothers would cook all sorts of scrumptious dishes. Christmas was the holiday that most excited us. Cari and Bill would stay up late after we had gone to bed and stuff our stockings, put the presents under the tree, and hang angel hair on the Christmas tree to signify the angels' visit. I really think they loved making the holidays fun for us kids. And because of that, the holidays were always memorable.

We didn't watch a lot of television at the Wensleys' when we were little, except for the cartoons and the other kids' stuff on Saturday morning. I always loved Tom and Jerry, Abbott and Costello, Woody Woodpecker, Laurel and Hardy. But I never watched *The Brady Bunch*. When I got older, everyone used to sing the theme song, and I would think, *where was I when this show was going on?* Why did everybody else's family use the television as a babysitter while we watched television only when Bill or Cari was there with us? Eventually, the answer became obvious. We were in such delicate emotional health when we came to Bill and Cari that every show on the tube was a potential trigger for terror and hysteria. All I needed was to deal with the opening moments of *The Brady Bunch* when it was revealed that fate had left Mr. Brady and Mrs. Brady alone to take care of their children!

Besides, the Wensleys believed in controlling and censoring what their children watched. They were religious people, and as the years passed they became increasingly fundamentalist in their beliefs. There was no drinking, smoking, or cursing in our house. They felt the rest of the kids in America were being corrupted by television, and they had no intention of letting us sit in front of the boob tube and channel-surf on our own through the hot romances and the multi-murders of prime time. Many times if we were watching a movie with them and a kissing scene came on, we had to cover our eyes. Sometimes we weren't allowed to watch the rest of the movie.

Every Sunday we went to church and Sunday school at the Green Mountain Christian Center. Cari dressed us up like little angels. We had fancy dresses, patent leather shoes, bonnets with ribbon ties, and little pocketbooks. Eventually, Cari and Bill moved to the more rigid Missionary Alliance Church in Bennington, where the congregation shared their views on church–state relations and morality. We went to summer Bible school there. And when we started getting older, we went to evening services and youth group. We prayed before meals and before going to sleep.

I loved church. I didn't really think of the religion. I just loved hearing the Bible stories and playing games. We had a big kid's Bible at home, easy to understand, with big pictures and bold letters. Every night before we went to bed, my mother would read us a story from the Bible. Every once in a while my father would, too.

My mother.
My father.

Magic words.

I studied the Old and New Testaments and got prizes for being a good memorizer of verses. My favorite story was the story of Daniel in the lion's den, and my favorite picture was the one of the Last Supper.

I think that in a way, it was our family's religious standards that kept us from staying in touch with our brother Duane. Although he would always feel like Emma's child, Duane was beginning to settle down with a foster mother of his own, a teacher named Carol Wehner.

There was a real lifestyle difference between these two foster mothers who had inherited the care of our little family. Cari told our social worker that she felt Carol was "too buddy-buddy with Duane . . . too friendly, too down to his level, not *motherly*." And Cari especially objected to the fact that Carol had given Duane a tape of AC/DC for his birthday, which Cari felt was "satanic and very inappropriate." So without our knowing it, our brother was now moving to a household that our religious foster parents didn't really approve of, where they would not feel really comfortable sending us to play. Duane's own discomfort with memories of our early life together deepened the separation.

As time went by, we saw less and less of him.

Eventually we lost him completely.

Escape, Part 3

SIX MONTHS AFTER we settled at the Wensleys' house, a couple of social workers came over to see how we were getting on. What they saw made SRS very happy. We were beginning to thrive physically. My patchy, ragtag reddish hair was growing at last. Diana already had thick auburn braids. We were both talking clearly and freely and showed no signs of our old nervous hysteria. The house was calm and clean and disciplined; Bill hugged us when he came home from work. One social worker noticed that Cari's attitude had changed—from "it's only temporary foster care, so let's not get emotionally involved" to "we want to make these girls a part of our family permanently."

The Wensleys were everything SRS could have hoped for in a foster family. A worker named Catherine Cadieux was assigned to secure the separation of Emma's parental rights, and she assured Cari that when we were free for adoption, the Wensleys would have "first dibs."

I don't remember Catherine, but reading her reports, I feel she was probably one of the most important people in my life—and that Diana, Duane, and I were incredibly lucky to land in her caseload during some really crucial years. She was thorough and meticulous. She covered all the bases.

The day that Catherine Cadieux took over our case, December 19, 1980, she sent several letters to Emma at all her possible known addresses, telling her that SRS wanted to resolve our status once and for all. One of those letters somehow got through. When Emma called—semi-coherent, spouting paranoid delusions about how the social workers and the tenants upstairs were all out to get her—Catherine kept verbatim records to show her state of mind.

She wrote to Emma informing her that SRS was going to petition the court in late September 1981 to free Diana and me for adoption. It was really important legally that Emma should have every chance to get a lawyer and contest the termination. To make absolutely sure that she knew what was going on, the judge insisted that SRS have the message delivered to Emma by hand. So Catherine found a social worker in New York who did exactly that.

If ever Vermont stood in danger of losing on this separation of parental rights petition, the news from New York clinched a victory for sure. It turned out that Emma had given birth to another baby there and had abandoned this child in the parking lot of a hospital. Luckily, a woman who happened to be passing rescued the baby, who was soon adopted.

At the hearings on the separation of Emma's parental rights, Catherine came prepared with all her documents and affidavits, and Cari testified about our needs and our progress and said that she and Bill wanted to adopt us when we were free. Emma never showed. The court decided that her situation was marked by "stagnation coupled with a prospective inability for improvement," and we were remanded to the custody of SRS.

At last, we were free for adoption.

CHAPTER *Two*

WHEN I FLEW to Biloxi for the finals of the Miss Teen USA Pageant in June 1993, it was the first time that I had been in an airplane since coming to the States from Puerto Rico with Emma and Duane. When I got off the plane with the other girls in the New England contingent, the heat nearly bowled me over. I began to sweat. My hair frizzed. My face got all shiny. My dress had torn on the plane, so I had changed into another, which necessitated a change of shoes. But I didn't have the right shoes for the second dress, so I borrowed some from Miss Maine Teen USA and they were two sizes too big for me. I could barely walk in them. All my life, I had imagined that I—by nature and genealogy a Puerto Rican who had been misplaced by my mother in the snows of Vermont—would just love being dropped into a place like this steamy city on the Gulf Coast. What a mistake! Where were my Puerto Rican genes when I needed them? I felt like the runt of the New England contingent, dripping and tripping.

And then to make things worse, these girls from places like Oklahoma and California arrived, looking as if they had just flown in from Vidal Sassoon.

I had one of the conversations with myself that I've been having since I was a toddler. *I don't care!* I said to myself. *If they don't like me because my shoes are too big and my hair is frizzy and my face is shiny, and that's all they're going to judge me on, then that's okay because I didn't want to be Miss Teen USA anyway!*

But then the Marines showed up to carry our bags and escort us to—don't laugh, this is true!—a Rice-a-Roni train, which was like a tourist bus that rode us through the town. Heads turned in the streets. Everyone was looking at us. Cameras were everywhere. We were treated like royalty. We had bodyguards and chauffeurs and police escorts named Brian and Bob and Joe, who are the best cops in the world and just loved stopping traffic so we could go by. My attack of toddler heebie-jeebies vanished. Who cared about the heat? This pageant was already turning out to be a lot of fun!

As soon as we arrived at our hotel, we had things to do. We had to get fitted for our "fun suit," our dance production outfit. We all got sneakers, high heels, makeup. We had pictures taken in our swimsuits.

I checked in and met my roommate, Miss Florida Teen USA. She was very pretty, with olive skin, dark eyes, dark hair, and high cheekbones. She was sort of medium-sized like me and very friendly and kind. As the week went by, she told me about her life and I told her about mine. She felt sympathetic toward me because I was a foster child and had overcome obstacles to get to the pageant. I felt sympathetic toward her because her parents had been divorced. She was very helpful to me with makeup, with which she was absolutely brilliant and about which I'd thought I knew a lot but now realized I knew totally nothing.

Sure, I was tense and nervous. We all were. But I had a system for dealing with my tension by now that I had developed in foster care. It's called music. I would listen to the soul and folk music of the URB brothers as they told stories about escaping from Estonia and coming to the States to find a better life. I would listen to Pink Floyd's hypnotic melodies and Van Morrison's mellow soul music. I would listen to Aerosmith sing about seeing the light, about how you're trying to survive out in the streets, trying to make it through, and one day you see the light and know everything's going to be all right.

I would sit in the room when my roommate wasn't there and sing, and I'd be okay.

At the Wensleys' House

I LEARNED THAT I could sing and perform at the Wensleys' house. I see myself growing up there in a series of scenes, plucked from the years like a bunch of flowers.

Their house opened out onto a lawn that rolled over to a huge pine forest. Behind the back yard there was an old field, a heavenly playland of high grass and pink thistle blossoms and Queen Anne's lace and darting butterflies. We had a big deck out back and a little fenced-in area where Cari kept ducks. Diana and I used to get up early in the morning, put on our little floppy garden hats, and scamper outside in our bare feet. I still remember the feeling of the cold, dew-soaked grass between my toes.

I would run into the woods and work on my tree house, which I built in a clearing among towering pine trees. I could reach it by crawling through an archway of low-lying boughs. My little house was all natural. I built pretend tables and chairs and planted a pretend garden. We had a lot of mountain black-berries and raspberries, so I could make pretend pies in my pretend kitchen. This was my haven, my very own spot, all mine, where no one needed to give me permission to come in, and no one could tell me to leave.

Every second I could I spent outside. I believe my impulse to always be outdoors was a reaction to the time when we'd been with Emma, and we were always locked inside dingy rooms. Diana and I would pick big bouquets of wildflowers and bring them home to Cari. Once she and Bill went to Massachusetts, and they bought a picture because they said it looked just like Diana and me in the meadow. And they were right! I swear, the artist had to have seen us to paint that picture. Two little girls in a field picking flowers—one with red hair and tan skin and one with brown hair and pale skin. The smaller one had a white hat on, and they both wore checkered shorts like the shorts Bill and Cari had bought for us.

Another one of our favorite things was the cardboard boxes that would be left behind when something got delivered. We would get into those boxes, close them, and roll down the hill over and over until the boxes were shredded. Or I would drag one around with me in it, holding it around me as if it were my car.

I wasn't hard to please.

Give me a cardboard box, and I was set for a day.

As kids, we would trek through the old logging trails that surrounded our neighborhood. It was exciting, because we never knew what we might find at the end of the trail. Once we found a huge sand pit, so we dragged sheets out of the house and attempted to parachute off the sand dunes. At the end of another trail, we found a beautiful beaver pond. When I was in third grade, there was a nature poster on the wall beside my desk that reminded me of that pond. I was often caught gazing dreamily at the poster, wishing that instead of being in school, I could be running through the woods toward the gleaming, sunlit water.

The Incredible Adventures of Clinnondale

WE ESPECIALLY LOVED it when Bill Wensley, our new father figure, would tell us one of his famous "Clinnondale" stories, about this guy Clinnondale who Bill said was his grandfather and had traveled all over the world and had all these adventures. Of course, they were all made up, but we thought they were the God's honest truth. The stories would always start out exactly the same way: "One day Clinnondale was sitting in his office with his partner . . . and all of a sudden, the phone rang . . ." And we would go, "Aghhh! there it is! that ringing phone! It's the start of something big! Come on, Papa, what happens next?"

And it would always happen that Clinnondale and his partner were being sent on a mission to some exotic foreign place and there would always be a title for the stories like "The Hunt for the Hidden Red Ruby." Right away, Clinnondale would have to fly off to Africa or some other wonderful place and ride an elephant. Bill would get into all kinds of graphic detail about what it was like to ride an elephant, how you sat, where you held on, and how you got the elephant to stop when he was running amuck because he had been scared by a loud sound, and Diana and I would yell and laugh, "Oh yeah, Papa, like you really know how to ride an elephant! So tell us more, what happened then?"

The wily antagonist of all these stories was the Black Panther. Bill had a way of turning down the lights and whispering as Clinnondale crept through the jungle.

"The wet slithery leaves of the jungle bushes tickled his face in the pitch dark. His feet sank into the bog on the jungle floor. Squish. Squish. He felt like somebody was watching him. But who could it be? And then, all of a sudden, he turned around and . . ."

Bill would make a great panther sound.

"HISSSS! GROWL!"

And we would scream.

"AGGHHHH!"

And Bill would yell, "It was the dreaded Black Panther, breathing right down Clinnondale's neck!"

In the climax of the story, Clinnondale would always be falling down a pit or some other perilous, scary thing. Would he get out? Would he make it back to his office? Would the Black Panther beat him to the hidden red ruby? Bill would always stop right at the most exciting part, saying, "Well, it's time to go to bed now. I guess we'll have to wait and see what happens tomorrow."

Gradually, the stories and the sunshine and the beautiful trees and the big yard and the caring people began to have an effect.

I started loving the Wensleys.

I started needing them.

The period of "initial testing" ended and gave way to a period of wanting their love and approval that lasted for years—that lasted forever.

Leftover Terrors

ONE DAY, THE Wensleys decided to paint our room, so our beloved bunk beds were moved away from the walls. Diana and I went bananas. The beds were a symbol of our new security! If the beds were moved, we might be moved next! We started screaming in the middle of the night again, falling out of bed. I would dream that men were coming to get Diana and take her away. Our social worker, Catherine, looking for some way to reassure us, suggested that pending the final adoption, the Wensleys might want to sign a long-term foster care agreement, which would give us some sense of stability.

Bill and Cari responded right away.

"Cathy's coming over to bring a piece of paper that will keep you with us for a long, long time," Cari said.

That was all it took. Suddenly, our foster parents reported, we were all smiles and sparkling eyes. We looked at them directly—not furtively—for the first time.

We were full of questions.

"What happens if Emma comes?" we asked.

Cari walked across the room and locked the door.

"You mean you won't let her in? You mean you won't let her take us?"

Cari hugged us and held us in her lap.

"How come God let me go to Emma's first instead of here?" I wanted to know.

Cari explained that Emma was sick now, but that maybe she hadn't been so sick back when she first had us.

And anyway, she said, it was sometimes hard to figure out God's purposes.

The Busiest, Prettiest Mother in Vermont

IN THOSE DAYS, when Cari was raising Billy and her new baby, Laura, Diana and I were both in nursery school, and Bill was just getting started in the insurance business, money and time and space were all pretty tight. We lived in a mostly rural state where nothing was within walking distance, so Cari was always driving one of us someplace. Whenever she got where she was going, she could barely catch her breath before she had to go out and drive again.

Even with four kids to care for, Cari tried to work part-time. First she became an Avon lady. Then she began teaching an evening class at church. We all shared the household chores; Saturday was cleaning day. I remember we used to gossip while we cleaned the toilets. We had to do our laundry as soon as we could reach the buttons on the washing machine.

We four kids all slept in one room, and as we got bigger that room grew smaller. The house was going to need a big addition to hold the family comfortably, and that loomed on the horizon, an ever-present oncoming expense. So frugality was the name of the game. As foster parents, Cari and Bill were entitled to be reimbursed for many expenses incurred on behalf of Diana and me. But those expenses had to be recorded, submitted, authorized, and otherwise subjected to scrutiny by SRS. All the bureaucratic forms and interventions guaranteed that our foster-ness would remain vivid in the minds of our new parents.

In July 1981, Cari took me for a psychological evaluation that was required as part of the official separation from Emma. She did my hair in bows and barrettes, and she bought me beautiful shoes and a pretty dress. I even had a little pocketbook. And she got dressed up, too. In a state where many of the women dress for a rugged, rural life, Cari Wensley was a total knockout. She wore high heels! And her hair upswept! And would you believe it, *jewelry!* To me, she was the prettiest mother in Vermont.

But to the psychologist who was making the evaluation—who was probably accustomed to the more prevalent outdoorsy types—Cari seemed overdressed. And he thought I was overdressed, too. His report was not flattering.

But it was important to *me* to look terrific. I mean, I walked down the street and met a kid who had known me before I came to the Wensleys, and she cried out, "Look! Charlotte's got hair!" I was so mortified! By putting me in ribbons and bows, by keeping me clean and neat, by looking beautiful herself, Cari drove away my demons and calmed some of my deepest fears.

July 30, 1981

ON JULY 30, 1981, the long-term care agreement was signed. It was a great day. We had a party at the Wensleys. We hung streamers from the kitchen ceiling and decorated the table. Catherine sat next to us on the couch and told us that we no longer had to worry about having to go and live with Emma. She said that soon we'd be going to court to ask the judge to make it possible for us to stay with the Wensleys forever and ever. And then we signed the papers. Even me. Even Diana, who was four years old and wrote her name in pencil with Bill's help.

Given what had happened to us so far, it was the most wonderful day of our lives.

You know, people say you start your life innocent, and then you start facing reality and see all the bad things that life brings. It was the other way around for my sister and me. We were *born* into reality—not sunshine and laughter and fun and games. After I had been with the Wensleys for a while, I began to see the good things that life brought. I started growing into my innocence.

When We Were Bad . . .

WHEN WE WERE bad at the Wensleys', we were punished. At the time, I never questioned whether it was right or wrong for us to be punished. I accepted it, and I accepted my guilt. However, I feel now that the cycle of guilt and punishment played a huge role in my relationship with them.

The Wensleys believed in spanking—not just a couple of swats. We had to go to our room and pull down our pants and our underwear. Then they would spank us with paddles really hard. These spankings were terrifying to me, probably because I had come from an abusive home. I was trying so hard to believe that the Wensleys loved me, but every time they spanked us, I felt that could not possibly be true.

We would often be spanked when we did something wrong. And there were so many things you could do wrong at the Wensleys'! You could see the wrong TV show, be friends with the wrong kid, eat the wrong food. And if you lied about doing those things, that was the wrong-est thing of all. Cari told us that lying was the biggest sin. If we lied, she said, we would be going down the path to the Devil and would turn out just like Emma! The very idea of that made me tremble. The stress of avoiding sin replaced the fun in life with the fear of fun.

Instead of growing closer to the Wensleys because I was learning to love them, I was growing apart from them because I was terrified of what they would do to me or say to me if they got angry. I needed a family situation in which I didn't have to worry whether they loved me unconditionally—where they would love me no matter what I said or did. But at this foster home, I felt a lot of tension in the air. Life with Emma had been like a weed-infested garden that was visibly out of order because it hadn't been properly cared for. At the Wensleys', I was living in a garden that looked neat and pretty and appealing. But if anyone had taken the trouble to look more carefully, they would have seen weeds of fear and mistrust that were suffocating the flowers around them, including me.

One time, Bill and Cari were going out. There was some cherry pie on top of the refrigerator. We were told not to eat it. When they came home, the cherry pie was gone. Bill and Cari were very upset and wanted to know who had eaten it. Clearly it was one of us kids, but who? I knew I hadn't done it. Diana, Billy, and Laura said they hadn't done it. The Wensleys got really mad. They thought we were *all* lying. They made us swear on the Holy Bible. We all swore. So they took us down to the basement and spanked each of us. We were crying and saying that we hadn't done it.

They continued to spank us until one of us would 'fess up. No one did. So they took out a bottle of stuff that they said would make us throw up so they would see clearly who had eaten the cherry pie. (We later learned it was just food coloring and water.) They made each of us swallow a spoonful. We all went into the bathroom, crying our eyes out, waiting to throw up.

Finally we calmed down enough to discuss the situation among ourselves, and we decided that this test of wills was going to go on indefinitely unless one of us took the rap. So Laura, who was the littlest and would get punished least severely, "admitted" that she had eaten the cherry pie.

To this day, I don't know who ate the pie. But it occurred to me that because it was left out without being covered, one of the cats could have eaten it.

Another punishment in our house was grounding—silence and isolation. One time, Diana was in the fifth grade and didn't do her homework assignment. She was supposed to bring home a pink slip for Bill to sign. At first she was too afraid to show

Bill the paper, so she found the signature stamp in his office and stamped his signature on it. But then she decided that was wrong, crossed out the stamped signature, and went to Bill to ask him to sign the paper. He yelled at her and spanked her, then declared that she had to stay in her room for two weeks. We couldn't see her or speak to her. She couldn't come downstairs to eat with us.

When I look back on it now, I know that the punishment didn't mean that the Wensleys didn't love us. Probably it was just the opposite. As fundamentalist Protestants, they believed in a set of iron-clad values, which included strict discipline.

The Performer Surfaces

I PROCESSED MY experience this way: We'd live in a home, the people really seemed to like me for a little while, and then I'd have to leave, so I'd think they didn't like me anymore. This worldview really affected me psychologically: when I was growing up—even when I was too little to understand—I *always* felt rejected.

But because she was one crucial year younger, Diana had worlds more confidence than I did. As Catherine wrote in her case notes, "Charlotte has low self-esteem and is much more self-conscious than Diana. Charlotte is willing to please, obedient, will do anything to make you happy, and is very sensitive to people's needs. Diana is more independent, less compliant."

To this day, I'm always worried about doing something that will turn off the people I care about and make them not like me anymore. Growing up, I'd look for approval all the time. I'd always try to be the best little girl, the one who brought pride and honor to the family. If you step back and think about that, you could say, "Wow, Charlotte! What a pathetic, needy little wimp you were!" On the other hand, there's an upside. My personality profile was absolutely ideal for somebody who would one day have a career in show business. I had the nervous system of a born performer. It bubbled up in me and Diana (and, as it turned out, in Duane too). A singing gene, music in the blood.

In second or third grade, I played a doctor in a school play. I had a lot of lines. I became terrified when I had to go on stage, but once I was out there, I absolutely loved it! Cari sent us to ballet lessons starting in second grade. I loved that, too. It meant everything for me to hear my teacher say, "Honey, you're wonderful!" At ballet school they were putting on a dancing play, *Cinderella,* and I got a really good part. But I needed a certain kind of leotard, with a certain kind of skirt and little dancing shoes, and it was all too expensive. So I couldn't be in the show, and I felt sad and disappointed.

The way we mostly got performing into our lives was in church. We heard Christian music all the time—Amy Grant was one of our favorites—and we memorized all the words. Diana was a really good singer and a lot more outspoken about wanting to sing than I was. I was afraid that if I said I wanted to do it too, I would look as if I was trying to copy her. So I never told anybody.

Then one Christmas—I guess I was about nine years old—I got a solo to sing in front of the whole church. It was hard, but I memorized it. I was afraid of screwing up and would practice and practice endlessly.

The minute I went on stage, my nervousness melted away completely. I was singing about Jesus being born, so I closed my eyes, imagining the hay in the manger and the cows mooing and the cold desert night in Bethlehem, and the baby Jesus in his little crib. I became so totally involved in imagining what I was singing about that the audience could feel what I was feeling.

"Oh, Charlotte," they said. "That was so beautiful! You showed so much expression. You sounded as if you really meant what you were singing."

I did.

That experience encouraged me to keep going, so I sang in the church's junior choir. They gave me quite a few solos. Soon Diana and I got to be known as "the Wensley Sisters Who Sing for the Church."

As we grew older, the entertainment thing began to feel more and more important to Diana and me. I wasn't shy about making up little skits to perform. Many of the skits were about situations that we had been through, like being separated from Duane and Emma, or situations that we hoped to be in, like getting some big award or being adopted. When I look back and remember myself playing out these situations, I see it as treating myself with my own therapy—to relive moments that were frightening, sad, or even vaguely remembered; to have control; to change the ending; to imagine the best. I know that it has helped me tremendously. Now that I'm taking acting classes, I see how similar those experiences were to my studies today.

Even though we couldn't watch *Hill Street Blues* like the other kids, and we rarely went to the movies because of what Bill and Cari considered the filthy language and the corrupting stories, we heard all the sweet stuff on the radio—the Beach Boys, Elton John, James Taylor, Seals & Crofts. We would go outside and stand on tree stumps and pretend we were Bette Midler. *You are the wind beneath my wingssssss!* The neighbors heard us and called out, "Sing it again, girls!" and the sound of everybody laughing and singing along with the Wensley Sisters rang out over the meadow and through the woods.

I know that these gifts could only have come from Emma and from our natural fathers, whoever they were. Some things only come from nature, not from nurture, and it's fascinating to me that all three of us—Diana, Duane, and me—are musical. I wonder about the other kids Emma gave birth to—whether they're out there singing and dancing someplace, too. No matter how much I feared Emma, no matter how much I held against her, I always felt tied to her by music in the blood . . . and that was a great comfort to me. It helped me survive in foster care, because it was a way of knowing that I was really someone's real daughter and that at least something I had received by nature from her was positive.

The Wensleys helped to fan the natural flame by giving us piano lessons. I lasted about two years. Diana, who is a much more patient and thoughtful musician, stayed with it a lot longer. She writes songs, Diana. She just sits there and works it through until it's right. She has written over forty songs, some about our brother, some about me. She's really talented. She'll make it big someday. I know she will.

Jesse the Cat

IT WAS NOT so easy for me to make friends with the other kids. I hadn't learned many social skills at the Wensleys' house. The only person I was close to was my sister, and even she bothered me. I was always afraid to get close to anybody, I guess because of a deep rooted fear that they might abandon me.

But I did have one wonderful friend: a cat named Jesse. He was one of three who lived in our house. Jesse was a Persian, with dark hair. I basically took him over when I moved in. He became my best friend. When everyone else was playing with other kids, I was playing with Jesse. He was so lovable! He'd sit on my neck and follow me everywhere. I would talk to him and he would start meowing as if he were really talking back. When

I was unhappy, he would lick my face. He was the best cat in the whole world.

When I was about ten years old, we got into a big problem with Jesse. He started to pee on the side of the house, to mark his territory, and then he started peeing in the house, too. Maybe there was something wrong with him; maybe he was sick. But whatever it was, Bill declared that he wasn't allowed inside anymore.

I was devastated and took this banishment personally. Even though I wasn't being rejected, the creature closest to me in the whole world was being rejected. It was wintertime. Freezing. The longer he stayed outside, the more he peed. I think he was just like one of us kids, acting up to get attention. I hated seeing him out in the cold. It brought back horrible memories of the days with Emma. Every day, I would get bundled up and go outside and hold Jesse close to warm him. It got to the point where the weather was so cold that Cari couldn't stand Jesse's suffering, and she let me sneak him into my room.

But it was too late. Jesse was sick unto death and down for the count. They put him to sleep one day while I was at school.

He was my cat, Jesse. I loved him. I told him everything. He was like my diary. He was the first friend who I felt never rejected me.

Human Friends: They Come and Go

MOST OF BILL'S and Cari's friends were from the Missionary Alliance Church in Bennington, and our friends were supposed to be church people too. I loved church in those days: the singing, the prayers, the security. But as I got older, I longed for a taste of the outside world. And in the tiny universe of our congregation, that could mean the next block. When I was in the fourth and fifth grades, I made a couple of friends who did manage to teach me about the outside world, even though they were only ten years old and we were just playing.

One friend was Sally. Her mother and father were very devout Christians but still not as strict as Bill and Cari. In her house, I learned that there was more than one way to be close to God, that you didn't have to be so radical or so afraid of sinning, and that you could live a normal life. Another girl I played with was Francie the Farmer. Her family had a big spread with horses. She wasn't religious at all and thought our family was totally weird.

My other friend was April, an athletic, redheaded girl who lived down the road. We would thunder up and down the length of our development on our bikes and go running through the woods on the trails that led to the beaver ponds. When Cari wanted us home for dinner, she would ring a big cowbell, and I would wave goodbye to April. Then Billy and Diana and I would all come charging in from all over to eat.

But there was more to April than fresh air.

Her mother was divorced. She worked as a waitress and was almost never around because she spent her time going out and having fun. April's two older sisters were party animals. They taught her all the good fashions and all the cool music, which she played on her boom box. And all I could listen to was the Beach Boys and Christian soft rock!

I used to think it was so cool that her mom let her swear. I couldn't say "Oh my gosh!" April said "Goddammit!" and "What the hell!" She knew what a menstrual period was way before we needed to know. She was playing Spin the Bottle when I didn't even know what Spin the Bottle was! She could go to movies! With our family, it was Walt Disney or nothing. Once, our whole family went to see a movie with John Candy and Chevy Chase, and I remember sitting there loving it. But then suddenly we had to leave, because the raccoons who were eating

John Candy's food were having a conversation shown in sub-
titles, and some of the words were profane.

I so wanted to go to the movies with April and her sisters. I
tried to bring up the subject with Cari and Bill, but the answer
was always "No, no, no!"

Although she was just eleven years old, April had already
filled out in front. She always wore bras and pretty underwear.
I was a scrawny twig, a full year or two behind in growth,
wearing sturdy cotton underpants and undershirts. (Eventually,
in junior high, I got so crazed from being flat-chested that I
stuffed my bra with cotton. Diana showed me how. For a tom-
boy who was supposed to be Miss Goody Two-shoes, my kid
sister always managed to know the score.)

Cari wanted us to be happy with our appearance. She believed
in that kind of satisfaction. She bought me my first blush and
my first lipstick in the fourth or fifth grade. The very next day I
wore it. But then she must have had second thoughts, because
when I came home, she told me she had had a dream where God
had told her I was too young and that it wasn't right for me to
be wearing makeup. So she put a tiny bit of blush on my cheeks,
but the lipstick went into a drawer and didn't come out again
for a couple of years.

In my friend April's house, there were no second thoughts.
She had lipsticks in every color.

No no no!

April danced. I didn't know how to dance. Dancing was too
provocative, too sexy.

No no no!

I see from my files that Cari was concerned that I had be-
friended a little girl who was a bad influence on me. So I guess
she may have known I was lying when I said, "I'm going over
to April's to watch *The Care Bears* and *Rainbow Bright!* Bye,
Mom . . ."

. . . when really we were going to gorge on Twinkies and chili dogs and watch *Nightmare on Elm Street.*

As I progressed into sixth and seventh grades, the friends I had grown up with—April and Sally—just dropped me. All of a sudden, when they got to the age when kids start thinking about who you are, where you were born, and what you look like, I wasn't cool. They had started to grow and I was stagnant. They didn't want to know me anymore.

They left me out of things.

They ignored me in school.

I was terribly hurt. But I would cling to them and try to deny they were dropping me, because I didn't have anybody else and I didn't want to be alone. For me, to be alone without friends was worse than anything else. I was on the playground one day, and a boy turned to me and narrowed his eyes and wrinkled his nose and asked, "Why are you here? Why are you hanging around with us?"

"I'm here 'cause these are my friends," I answered.

He just laughed and walked away.

The only friend who stuck with me was Francie the Farmer, the one with the big spread and the secular family. She was friends with April and Sally, and she still stayed friends with me. I thought, *That's what it means to be really accepted—you can afford to be nice to everybody.*

Family Models

Every year we would go off to a big outing in Massachusetts for the families of salespeople who, like Bill, worked for the insurance company. I loved these events, because they gave me a chance to see how other kids lived, how they interacted with their families, what they owned, how they dressed, what rules they lived by. I was always doing that—comparing my life with someone else's. I always felt that other kids had it better than Diana and me. My major emotion was jealousy. Not mean, dangerous jealousy, but the aggrieved, longing kind of jealousy that is sort of benign and sad.

I was totally envious of our cousin, Colleen.

Her mother—Aunt Sarah—was a fashion model. She was my inspiration.

She was tan and slender and blonde and married to a Greek shipping captain. Colleen was their only child. She was beautiful like her mother, dark like her father. We saw them once a year. They lived on a boat! Colleen had a tiny room, like a closet, with two bright blue hanging beds and a zillion toys. And the kitchen was the size of a booth at Wendy's!

As far as I could see, Aunt Sarah worshipped Colleen. I remember her sweet, soft voice calling, "Colleen, it's bathtime. Colleen, it's time to eat, honey." By my standards, that made Colleen the world's luckiest girl. Cari Wensley didn't coddle and cuddle and spoil. We rarely got individual attention; there were just too many of us. We were transported, fed, educated, and cleaned as though we were "the troops." But Aunt Sarah took Colleen's hand, washed her face, brushed her hair, asked how she felt—and that seemed so fabulous to me, a special tenderness. Of course, the grass is always greener, right? When Colleen got older, she said that she felt stifled by her mother's attentions and envied us because Cari didn't hover over us all the time.

We had so much fun with Colleen. Whenever she would visit, we'd put on a show. One year, we pretended we put together a trio called CDC (Charlotte, Diana, and Colleen) and did a funny Motown blues number with screwy lyrics that cracked up the family.

I never saw Bill laugh so hard.

I loved that feeling—making people laugh. It made my heart sing.

Because Aunt Sarah was a model, there was a precedent in the family, and Cari encouraged me to go into the same line of work. As long as I didn't model lingerie, it was fine with her. When I was in middle school, the Wensleys told me they were going to send me to the Barbizon Modeling School. I was so excited. When it didn't happen, I kicked myself for getting my hopes up.

When I was in ninth grade, there was a model's talent search being held in a hotel in Albany, New York (which was nearby). I know now that many of those "searches" are often scams that are trying to get you for all you're worth, but at the time it seemed like a perfect start in my quest to be discovered. My friend Marcy and I decided to try it, and Cari agreed to drive us to the hotel, which was an hour and a half away. Marcy and I, very excited, dressed up in her clothes—black pants and tops to make us look as thin and tall as possible (not that either one of us needed any help at that point). I decided I wouldn't be wearing my hideous Coke-bottle glasses that night, and instead put on some eye makeup and lipstick. Cari was very impressed with both of us, and so were the judges, because we were supposedly two of only six that were selected from among tons of people. When it was my turn, I sat down at a table and spoke with a man and a woman. They were very nice and they seemed to like me. Then they had me speak in front of a video camera. It was exciting. I forgot about my nervousness and just enjoyed the experience. However, when Cari and Marcy's mother learned how much the project was going to cost ($200 for portfolio, head shots, etc.), they decided against it. Marcy and I toyed with the idea of trying to raise the money, but we then decided it wasn't worth it.

Cari and Diana and I talked endlessly about makeup and hair and fashions. We never missed a beauty pageant on television: Miss America, Miss Universe, Miss Teen USA. Cari always told me how beautiful I was going to be. She made me feel really good about myself in that respect. I groomed myself in anticipation. I had no idea how tall I would be, so all I could do was take care of my face, my teeth, my skin. I washed my hair every morning, washed my face twice a day, and brushed my teeth three times a day. I never had a cavity in my life. It was such a great feeling to know that I was getting a second chance at a strong body and a healthy life.

I was also quite a bookworm in those days. Books inspired me. It was so nice to read about other girls like me who were going through their own hard times and finding ways to have a happy ending. Darcy in *Homecoming,* V. C. Andrews' heroines —all those girls were being rejected because of who they were or where they had come from, and they had to fight to keep their dignity and rise above those who were trying to destroy them. They went through so much pain and heartache, but they always kept pushing. They all believed that there was something better in life for them to look forward to, if they could only press on past the bad times.

One year, Bill bought the family a camcorder for Christmas. Diana and I were dying to use it, and finally they let us. The first thing we did was to make our own fashion modeling videos. We even made credit frames: *Produced by Charlotte. Directed by Diana. Music by Kenny G.*

I would model and twirl around and play to the camera, and Diana would fade the music in and out. Sometimes during that period, while we shot those videos and I was just entering adolescence, I came upon the notion of being a star. I wanted to be known far and wide, in California and New York and Montana —all over the world! If I was an actress and I was on stage performing and people were applauding, then that was proof that they really loved me. I knew I could live off that! It was the ultimate reassurance, a Magic Kingdom of approval and free-dom and acceptance and control—my childhood playhouse in the pine trees, expanded to include the whole world. Every time I performed in front of a group of people and they loved it, that made me so happy! It was the best feeling I ever had.

I wanted that feeling never to go away.

The Clotheshorse Takes a Stand

THE IMPORTANCE OF money—and of making our own money —was instilled in us early. As kids we would make crafts to sell to the neighbors or sell our chickens' eggs. By the time we were nine and ten, we were buying our own toiletries. In the sixth grade, Diana and I each received a clothes allowance. I remem-ber it as about $50 for the winter, another $50 for the summer. The next year it was increased. Other items came directly from our parents as they were needed. For example, we received party dresses and sports equipment. I would babysit all the time to help buy the rest of my clothes. One time I needed a new pair of tennis shoes because the old ones had holes in them, and the Wensleys told me, "Save up your babysitting money and you'll be able to buy new ones for yourself."

I really thought that wasn't fair. I wanted to buy a bike with my babysitting money. I felt I shouldn't have to spend it on clothing. I looked at the girls at school, who didn't seem to be any richer than we were, and it seemed to me that they didn't have such severe limits on money for clothes. Their moms took them shopping and got them everything they needed, and when they grew out of that or wore it out, their parents saw to it that they had something new. I began to feel that the Wensleys weren't providing for us the way "real" parents would have and that my feelings were just not important to them.

At one point, I remember, I was so desperate for stuff to wear that I would sneak up into Cari's room and take her clothes and wear them to school, because I felt that I didn't have enough clothes of my own to get me through the week. I'd get home before she did and put them back in her closet.

It wasn't just preadolescence that made me desperate for clothes. It was that something had started happening to me.

About the middle of seventh grade, I stopped being dorky and started to *blossom*. Other girls started wanting to be my friend. Boys began to notice me. I began to feel good about myself. Along with my new popularity came one of the major jokes of girlhood. Some girls who had stopped disliking me because I was a nerd now started disliking me because I might possibly take away their boyfriends.

The truth is, I was so happy to have girlfriends that I wouldn't have looked crosswise at anybody else's boyfriend. But most middle school girls are so nervous about their acceptability that they are incapable of realizing that other girls are just as scared and insecure as they are.

The more popular I became at school, the more lost and unhappy I became at home. There were so many things I wanted to talk about, but they were forbidden topics in our house. Sex. Boys. The World. Evil. Money. Power. The World. Sex. When you're really young, you just want to play. They feed you and you love them and they love you. But then when you get older, and you want to talk about more mature things, and you have opinions of your own, you're not so easy to take. I didn't want to pick flowers or play war on my bunk bed anymore. I wanted to go to movies and to dances, to learn about society and the real world. Bill and Cari were afraid we were going to get bad morals from those things, so they said we couldn't go out with any boys unless they were from the church. But I didn't like any of the boys from the church.

I didn't want to be close-minded and lead a secluded, sheltered life full of regret and longing to do all the things I wasn't allowed to do. I wasn't asking to do anything immoral or illegal. I was just asking to be allowed to grow up according to my own individual style, to have some control over my own life. Why couldn't I communicate with my parents the way my friends could? Why couldn't I be allowed to make my own mistakes like everybody else and learn from them and *grow up?*

It was ridiculous. And if I tried to talk about it, I got nowhere. To get anywhere, to do anything, I had to commit the biggest sin: I had to lie.

There was a distance between me and my foster parents, and it was becoming more pronounced as I got older and needed to communicate more. Were they afraid of becoming too close, of neglecting their natural children? Did they have a lingering suspicion of our background? I always felt the distance, but I never understood its source.

WHEN I WAS almost thirteen, Cari did a great thing. For seven weeks she drove us all across the country with a van and an RV trailer all hooked together. Bill was too busy to start out with us, but he joined us later on. We went all the way through Kansas, Nebraska, Colorado, the Rocky Mountains, Idaho, Mesa Verde, Bryce Canyon, Yellowstone, Zion, the Grand Canyon. We went all through California, from the southern tip to the northern border. Universal Studios. Santa Barbara. Redwood National Park. We drove up the Oregon Coast and met a cousin in Seattle. We spent the Fourth of July in Las Vegas. I don't think I ever loved Cari and Bill Wensley more than I did on that trip, because I was old enough by now to appreciate how wonderful it was to have parents who believed in education, who believed in travel and exposing their children to the glories of nature.

On the way, though, Diana and I had a major confrontation with the Wensleys. It was about the clothing dilemma. We were in a national park in California. And we finally got up the nerve to approach Cari and say that we needed more money for school clothing. There was a big argument. But we won. When we got home, for the first time, we began receiving our monthly state clothing allowance directly. I was filled with the sudden thrill of independence. At last I had some control over how I looked.

However, with this instant infusion of money, it really dawned on me that I was not like other kids. My clothes didn't come from Mom and Dad. They came from the state. I had not been adopted. I was still "foster." I could actually be tossed out if I was bad. On the other hand, I could leave if I wanted to, and somebody would still take care of me.

Foster-ness.

The feeling of not quite being in solid.

The sense of noncommitment.

The state of temporary.

CHAPTER *THREE*

As we approached the big night of the Miss Teen USA Pageant in Biloxi, Mississippi, we wised up to the weather and learned to do our jogging during the cooler hours of the day. Some of the girls would sprint around the pool for exercise. Although I had been a runner starting in my sophomore year in high school, I hadn't been working out for the past six months because of a pulled Achilles tendon. I badly needed to get back in shape. So every morning, early enough to beat the heat, I'd get together with a whole bunch of the other girls to go jogging.

We had rehearsals from nine to five. Tad was the choreographer. Bob and Michelle were the young dancers who guided us. They were so charismatic! They made our dance rehearsals so much fun! There were scouts there from the modeling agencies, and maybe from the talent agencies too. Everyone was on edge —we all felt that people were inspecting us already.

When we started rehearsing on stage, I met Ken, the stage manager, who has become a real buddy of mine. I've run into him three times since we first met. He was the stage manager for Miss Teen USA, for *Star Search* with Ed McMahon, and for the Worldwide Kids Party that I attended. The thing about backstage people is that if you just take the time to appreciate them (which almost no one does), you realize that they are the ones who make everything happen. Also, to be truthful, I felt slightly intimidated by many of the other contestants who came from wealthy homes and had arrived with extraordinarily expensive clothing. I felt more comfortable with the blue-collar people backstage, because they appeared to be closer to the socioeconomic class I had joined when I left the Wensleys and went to live in the group foster care home in Bennington.

At the end of the day, we had dinner and always went to a party with our chaperons. Mine was Rose from Los Angeles, Mexico, Florida—everywhere. She cracked us up; I loved her. Don Seideman, the photographer I had met at the Vermont State Pageant, showed up again and took all kinds of pictures of me, then gave me an album as a special gift. What a treasure!

The city of Biloxi threw one affair after another in our honor. The first function was a big party at the hotel, with all the bigwigs from the Miss Universe Pageant. One time we went to the mayor's house, another to an Indian barbecue. It was so hot and humid—swamp wet. We went up a walk with torches on either side. We felt so celebrated and special. We were sitting on the lawn watching Indian chants and dances, and then red ants got into everybody's shorts and gave people itches and rashes, but we were having such a ball, we didn't mind. Of course, the pageant organization invited guys wherever we went. There was a DJ and dancing outside. We'd dance, sit down, dance again, and sit around, brushing away the red ants and fanning ourselves with paper plates like Southern belles. Another time, we went to a masked ball where we held the masks up in front of our faces the way they used to do in the olden days in Europe. We were introduced wherever we went. We walked down a runway and had our pictures taken. I got a lot of compliments on my outfit—a long plum skirt with a slit up the side and a plum vest, all in silk. And that made me feel great.

We had so much fun dancing, making friends. I love meeting new people. If I could, I would personally meet everybody in

America. There has always been something so fascinating to me about people who are different from me, who come from far-away cities and have acquired exotic kinds of knowledge. Even when I was a kid, I was always reaching out beyond the town where we lived, beyond the church, beyond our religious system to meet "the others" and do the unusual.

I think of this quality in me as a lust for experience and variety and just plain fun. But at one point in my life in the foster care system, it was called rebellion.

The Clever Lunatic

IN THE SPRING of 1987, Emma Caraballo wrote us a long letter. It had a tremendous impact on me, because it was all about culture. Ethnic roots. As I trudged to school in the April thaw, the snows melting into mud around me, I imagined the sound of Spanish guitars and the heady aroma of fat pink blossoms in lush Puerto Rican gardens. What a clever lunatic she is, old Emma!

She said her middle name was Zoraida, which she insisted was the family name of a princess in a royal kingdom in medieval Spain. "And so I was not that princess of the past," she wrote, "but now in these days a mother who remembers you and your sister very much and also loves you very much."

She said our grandmother's name was Maria, that our grandfather's name was Alfonso, that they were good, loving parents to her, and that because of them we had Spanish and French blood. "I have missed you all the time we have not been together," she wrote. "I have always wanted to get together with you again." And then there was a picture of a plump woman with a big smile, wearing a white and black coat.

She looked a lot like me.

We had the same mouth, the same hair and skin coloring.

Cari told our new adoption worker—Lydia, who had come onto our case in addition to our social worker—that as a result of the picture and the letter, Diana and I were in an uproar. But I remember no such thing. No nightmares, no terror. Only a pure, burning curiosity. Should we meet Emma? Should we not? What would she be like? Would she try to take us away? I was in the sixth grade at that point, and the only fear I had of Emma was that I would turn out to be like her. It was my greatest fear in life. I saw myself being possessed by demons, going crazy, babbling incoherently to people who weren't there, drinking, becoming homeless, begging on the streets, and—the most terrible nightmare of all—*losing my family.*

It is possible that Cari may have shared my fear that I would turn out like Emma. In fact, just about the time I started giving her trouble, it seems Cari apparently started picking up on Emma's story that we were the daughters of demons. She sat us down and told us in all seriousness that it was possible Emma's story might be *true!* She bought a paperback book with demons pictured on the front cover, with claws and tails, horrible fangs and fire coming out of their mouths, and we all read it together. My sister and I were fascinated.

When the people who have been your parents for ten years—and taught you everything you know—suddenly start telling you that yes, it is possible that you are the children of demons, well . . . you kind of believe it. They were saying, well, you *are* left-handed, Charlotte, and you *do* have really light eyes, and Diana has this *strange* coloring, too, with the red hair and the brown skin. And instead of being revolted, my sister and I were kind of excited: *Wow! Cool!*

Of course, it wasn't cool. It was horrible.

Even so, the narrowness of life in the church had begun to oppress me. And just the idea that we weren't *naturally* part of the church, that the church wasn't our whole life, that we actually might be from the other side was like—this may sound totally crazy but it's true—a relief.

As summer approached, the adoption worker saw Emma in Bennington. They had a pretty rational conversation about us and Duane. Then Emma asked Lydia to drop her off in a parking lot, and she just sort of wandered out of our lives once again. I see her in my mind's eye, with her shopping bags and distracted gaze: this pretty, round woman, hovering on the verge of insanity, occasionally lucid and sweet, wandering across a parking lot in Bennington, Vermont, far far from her hot tropical home and her own people, disappearing among the cars.

Just Like Real

WE TOTALLY FORGOT about Emma because we were so excited about the new addition to our house. Actually, it wasn't like an addition. It was like a whole new house, twice the size of the original. Before it was finished, we used to play tag on top of the narrow foundation walls that were at least ten feet off the ground! There were pegs sticking up all over, and we would have to jump over them as we were running away from the tagger. It was pretty dangerous now that I look back on it. But it was a lot of fun! The new addition had a great kitchen, a big deck, a lovely new master bedroom, and—most wonderful of all—a separate bedroom for each of us four kids.

Billy got a new sunny airy room. Laura got a new sunny airy room. Diana got our old room—the one we had all shared—all for herself. And I got a room in the basement with no window.

I felt hurt and shortchanged. I objected that Laura and Billy were always preferred. It was explained to me that they were the "real" children, that I must surely be able to understand that. So of course I said yes, I understood. But to be honest, I didn't. It was explained to me that even though nobody really owed me anything, I had been housed and fed and loved and cared for just like a real member of the family.

But "just like real" wasn't enough for me. "Just like real" was what was causing our problems.

I wanted to be adopted.

I kept waiting for it to happen.

I never managed to know our adoption worker very well, but I always felt she was a close ally of Cari and Bill and not much of a friend to me. Looking back now, I feel that she should have paid more attention to Diana and me and not focused so completely on the needs and desires of the Wensleys. I think that was a key factor in our not being adopted. However, now that I have read the records, I'm reminded of something wonderful that she did on her visit to the Wensleys in July 1987. She brought us a book and some picture postcards and maps of Puerto Rico. We sat around looking for my birthplace and other locations mentioned in the birth certificates that the Puerto Rican authorities had sent. Maybe this means nothing—but maybe it means that in her own quiet way, Lydia was trying to help me discover an outside identity that would strengthen me and sustain me when I finally had to come to grips with the fact that I was really not one of the Wensley kids, like Billy and Laura: that the beautiful new rebuilt and expanded house was not a home whose warmth and beauty belonged to me by right but a kind of upscale boarding facility where I was fortunate enough to spend some happy years.

When you start searching for your roots, anything helps. Demon fathers. Postcards from San Juan. Anything.

Grammy Returns

As if fate were conspiring to drive little wedges in my relationship with the Wensleys, another figure from the past suddenly appeared: Grammy Peterson.

I don't know what possessed Diana and me to contact the Petersons. Maybe it was the recognition that we had a pre-Wensley family. Maybe it was dissatisfaction with the family that we had. But we were going though the phone book one day, and we found them. Diana called. We were both on phones in Bill's office.

"Hello . . . is Mrs. Peterson there?"

"This is she."

"It is?"

"Yes. Who is this?"

Diana turned to me and said, "This was a mistake; we shouldn't have called her." But the lady on the phone had already figured it out.

"Charlotte? Diana? How are you?! Oh my God, it's Charlotte, it's Diana!"

She just freaked out. She told us that it hadn't been her choice to give us up, that she really liked us but that she had gotten pregnant and didn't have any money . . . well, that was ancient history now . . . what was important was that we had called and she was so happy to hear from us. Grammy was dying to see us, she said. She lived right close by, and she'd love to have us for lunch.

We ran to tell Cari.

"Mom, guess who we just talked to! Mrs. Peterson!"

We thought our foster parents would be happy, but they were furious. We felt terrible. But then Mrs. Peterson called. She wanted us to come to lunch with her and Grammy. How could anyone say no? I remember the day. Diana and I were fixing our hair and getting dressed and putting on makeup. We wanted Mrs. Peterson and Grammy to see that we had really turned out just fine. When they came to pick us up, we came running down the stairs. They just stared at us.

"My babies," Grammy murmured.

She burst into tears.

We went back to Grammy's house. She showed us the first baby pictures we had ever seen of ourselves. She took us shopping. She bought me a porcelain doll. It was beautiful, with long brown hair like mine. Grammy told me that soon after, she bought another but didn't send it for months and months.

I guess something made her afraid to get too close.

There's a notation in my files that Bill and Cari complained because Grammy had been sending cards on all occasions, buying presents. Cari reported that Diana and I were sorry we had ever called the Petersons and wanted to stop thinking about the past.

I can't remember, but if we did say that, we only did it to make Cari happy and to assuage her fears about the existence of someone else who actually cared about us and might want to take us away.

Kids are smart. They know what to say.

The Struggle We Didn't Know About

I SEE NOW that what was happening to me was the beginning of a major teenage rebellion, which would explode like pollen in July. When I was living through it, I thought the drama of my rebellion was mine alone. But when I gained access to my case files, I realized that behind the scenes, my foster parents and SRS had long been engaged in a kind of endless struggle over whether Diana and I should be adopted (roughly the SRS position) or whether we should remain in long-term foster care (roughly the Wensleys' position).

The word *adoption* had glittered in the background all through the legal steps that led to our separation from Emma, like an Oscar waiting to be collected by the winner. But when we were free, the Wensleys apparently had serious second thoughts. Adopting two impoverished kids was a huge financial commitment, which they feared they would not be able to afford.

One caseworker spelled out their concerns. After all, as we were getting older, it was going to be more and more expensive to take care of us. We might need braces. Who was going to pay for the orthodontia? If we remained in foster care, the state would. We looked to be bright kids—Diana particularly was turning out to be a brilliant student—and it seemed logical that we would go to college. Who would pay the tuition? If we remained in foster care, we were officially "poor" and were eligible for all kinds of scholarships that might elude us if we became the adopted children of a middle-class family. I see in the files that Bill also mentioned a question of inheritance to one of our workers. Perhaps he felt pressure to keep the Wensley estate in the "real" family.

I hated money so much. Everyone always talked about how great money was, but as far as I was concerned, all money was doing for me was pushing my foster parents away from me and my sister.

I eventually discovered that in the early eighties, SRS had presented the Wensleys with an ultimatum: either they would have to adopt us or we would be taken away and placed in the home of another family that would adopt us right away.

Another adoption worker took a more conciliatory view. She asked Catherine to find out whether the Wensleys would adopt us if SRS offered them subsidies. This setup apparently worked.

Our foster parents did not want to lose us, and they accepted the idea of a subsidized adoption. In February of 1984, the adoption packet was sent to the Wensleys. By December, no paperwork remained except the final signatures.

There was only one trouble.

As of October, Catherine Cadieux had left our case.

Our great defender, the woman who had diligently followed her checklist down to the bottom so that we could be eligible for adoption, had been appointed to the pulpit of a church and departed for holier work. I truly believe that my one real chance of being adopted by the Wensleys departed with her.

When Catherine left, it seems to me, a new era of "benign neglect" entered the SRS relationship with the Wensleys. There were visits. Meetings. Judicial reviews. Papers presented. Positions clarified. Years went by. 1986. 1987. In January 1988 the subsidy issues still lay on the table. How long would the subsidy last? At what rate? Until age eighteen? Until age twenty-one?

Diana and I didn't know about the debate that was going on, but I certainly felt some fallout from it, because adoption was getting to be one of my major obsessions. Cari had told Catherine that I asked about it all the time. I vividly recall receiving vague answers to my questions. One of them was "SRS lost the papers, but they're looking for them." I must have felt pretty uptight about this issue, because one day, when my brother Billy was shirking his work, I yelled at him, "You don't have to do chores because you were born here!"

If our foster parents had ever felt pressure to adopt from people in the church or the neighborhood, that feeling was effectively squelched by the widely held belief that we had indeed already been adopted long ago. I met people from our congregation who believed that we were adopted. When I talked to Duane's foster mom, Carol Wehner, it turned out that she believed it too. The machinery of gossip, the "what-will-the-neighbors-think?" pressure that is so typical of rural Vermont, never applied to our cases, because nobody knew there was anything to gossip about.

The truth as I see it is that the longer we weren't adopted, the harder it became for Lydia and her colleagues at SRS to suggest adoption. We were too profoundly and emotionally connected to the Wensleys. Insisting on adoption when they were apparently doing such a good job with us in permanent foster care had to seem to the social workers like busting up a happy home on a technicality. "It was a judgment call," said one of our caseworkers.

I wish someone had asked me whether I thought the call was fair.

Diane Sawyer, the TV journalist who interviewed me and the Wensleys for an episode of the newsmagazine *Turning Point* focusing on foster care, concluded that it was "subsidy issues" that kept the adoption problem from being resolved. I believe that her conclusion was correct. No deal could ever be worked out between SRS and the Wensleys that was acceptable to both sides. And by the time the negotiations failed utterly, it seemed much too late in the game to place us elsewhere.

Clearly, the Wensleys never understood how important adoption was to me. They loved us. They wanted to keep us. They felt that was enough. I believe that their position was based on the notion—shared by many people involved in foster care—that adoption is pretty much an empty ritual, a bureaucratic step up from foster care with no deep meaning in and of itself.

For me, nothing could have been further from the truth.

The commitment of adoption would have proved to me that I was loved regardless of financial considerations.

As for SRS, they were pretty helpless after a while. Commissioner Bill Young tried to explain how they ended up that way.

From the worker's point of view, here is a child that had a terrible infancy and toddler life, very traumatic, who was in a couple of foster homes, but now has been with the Wensleys for a significant period of time in her life. Things seem to be going well. She is with her sister. I'm sure the worker is thinking, I don't want to separate her from her sister. The Wensleys are talking about adoption, but are not sure. The worker thinks: what I care about is that this child's life is not disrupted. If I force the issue with the Wensleys and end up taking the child out of the home, I don't know if I'll be able to place them both together. I may do more harm than good.

If that's the way "the worker" felt, then I say it was because she failed to inform herself sufficiently. If anybody had been there really watching our growth at the Wensleys—and talking to Diana and me on a regular basis—then they would have seen that everything wasn't "going well." As I read some of these case files, I saw that the Wensleys were the only people whose comments were recorded. There was almost no comment from me or Diana about how we were feeling. The worker would come to visit; we'd be sent downstairs; we'd be greeted but never really engaged in discussion. I don't remember anyone from SRS getting into an in-depth conversation with either of us about what our life was like.

I feel that the failure of SRS to communicate directly with us played a huge role in the failure of my relationship with the Wensleys. Commissioner Bill Young once said, "Kids that seem to be okay don't get attention." When you're a good kid and you don't make any trouble—and the caseload is burdened with emergencies, such as physical abuse, sexual abuse, runaways, and juvenile delinquents—it's very easy for you to get lost in the system.

I was a good kid. So I got lost.

Very shortly, like my brother before me, I would discover a way to be found.

The Storm Gathers

WITH EVERY PASSING month, I was getting into deeper and deeper trouble with my foster parents. Diana was graduating from sixth grade at the top of her class and was the star in the school and church shows. I was flunking math and had to take it over in summer school. Cari complained to SRS that I wanted to be "on the phone twenty-four hours a day" and found ways to spend entire weekends at the homes of my friends.

What was really going on was that I was staying away because I wasn't happy at home and much preferred being in other people's houses.

My attitude was described as "nonchalant."

Right. I had concluded that was the only safe attitude to have. I certainly couldn't display my anger, raise my voice, defy parental authority. I felt that I had to constantly arrange myself to meet my parents' every expectation or fit their mood, that everything I said had to be premeditated, that I always had to appear to be bubbling over, happy-go-lucky, and cheerful—or else I would be accused of having a bad attitude. We had to always put on this air of being the perfect happy family, no matter what was really going on.

The thing that seemed to worry Bill and Cari most was my new friendship with a girl called Marcy Franklin. I met Marcy toward the end of seventh grade. She was exactly my height but bustier and hippier, and she had short curly blondish hair. She was outgoing and really cute, and she had lots and lots of older buddies from the upper classes. For some reason, she liked me.

What a comfort it was to have a good friend at last! I had somebody to eat lunch with, somebody to walk down the hall with, somebody pretty and popular whose friends became my friends.

Marcy thought I was lucky to have parents who tried to shelter me from every bad thing. She was often sad that her mother and father were very busy and had little time to do anything with her but buy her stuff like a VCR and a stereo and then leave again. Conversely, I envied Marcy because, since her parents weren't around so much, she had a lot of independence. In my jealous fantasy, they allowed Marcy to do absolutely anything she wanted. I envied her because she had a closetful of great clothes and a sophisticated older sister and a phone that rang off the hook because she had so much confidence and such great social skills that everybody wanted to be her friend—which was what I envied most of all.

The great thing about Marcy was that I could tell her the truth of my heart. I felt that my foster mother was great to sit down and talk to when the subject was harmless—clothes, makeup, careers. But if I had a problem at school, with a teacher or another kid, she'd say, "Charlotte, you had better clear that up real quick. I don't want to get a call from them." All my resentments against the old friends who had abandoned me, all my insecurities and desires—that wasn't okay to talk about. So I had to keep that stuff inside. After a while, all the things I wanted to talk about and couldn't talk about began to create a riot in my brain. I was ready to explode.

I would go downstairs and rave at my stuffed animals and scream silently at my mirror, and sometimes I would close the door and get the tension out by singing and dancing. I'd imagine that I was on stage and zillions of people were watching me. I would sing my heart out, and the tension would come out with the song.

If I was upset about something and walked around moping, Cari would get very annoyed, because she liked everybody to be happy. Then she would think about it and do something great, like taking Diana and me out shopping. And I'd say to myself, "Okay, she still loves me," and I'd forget all about whatever I was moping about. Until the next time.

My case files say I was under peer pressure. Sure I was! Who isn't at twelve and thirteen? I wanted to be like everybody else in school, go to the dances and the movies, go out with Marcy and the guys on the track team. Did that mean that I was turning into the spawn of Satan, some crazy wild woman? Why did we all have to pretend that we were such totally perfect sin-free people, when everybody knows no one is perfect? Why couldn't we discuss going out and having a good time? Hadn't my parents ever wanted to do that when they were young? I was absolutely sure they had! All I wanted to do was go to a dance, for God's sake—a lousy school dance!

The answer was almost always no.

Very often, Diana and I would get down in my room and argue about who was going to ask for what forbidden thing.

"You ask."

"No, you ask."

"Come on, please, Diana, I'll let you use my radio, please."

But generally it was me who ended up asking, probably because I was older and the one appointed by my place in the family to break the ice and introduce the idea of adolescence into our happy home.

I quickly found that it just wasn't welcome there.

Time Out for the Great Eighth Grade Dance

IT WAS A major coup when Cari relented in her opposition to dancing and let me go to the eighth grade formal. Marcy was going, and she got me a date with her date's friend, so how dangerous could it be?

Cari took me shopping at the mall and bought me a navy blue strapless bubble cocktail dress. She helped me with my makeup. Bill bought me a beautiful wrist corsage. They took me over to Marcy's house. She was wearing a beautiful flowered dress, and her aunts and uncles took pictures of us, oohing and ahhing and carrying on, and Bill made a video. We felt like movie stars. For me it was a chameleon Cinderella moment. Take off Charlotte's glasses, give her some blush and lipstick, dress her in taffeta, and—wow—dorkiness transformed!

The dance was at the junior high school in the cafeteria, with a DJ and strobe lights and teachers and chaperons. I remember that everybody was hanging around outside, and when we arrived, people seemed really impressed with us. What a great feeling that was! My date was tall and skinny, and we just danced the night away. But the most fun we had was gossiping about the other girls. That was a riot!

"Wow, look at that wicked tight dress!"

"Her boobs are totally falling out!"

"My God! Look at how BIG her hair is!"

When it was over, at about midnight, our dates couldn't really take us anywhere because they didn't drive. So they just went home. Then a guy Marcy knew who had a white Subaru drove up with a bunch of his friends and asked us if we wanted to go to a big party. We said "Yes!"

So we got in the car, and he handed me an Irish coffee. It was my first drink. It tasted awful. But I smiled to show I was enjoying myself. I remember thinking, *I'm okay, I'm not going to get drunk or anything and let these guys take advantage of me, because Marcy is here and she will protect me because she knows how to handle these situations.* So we're driving around and they're passing the bottle and picking up this one in Bennington, dropping off that one in Shaftsbury, and of course it turned out that the big party which was supposed to happen never did happen, and finally everybody got tired and went home.

We ended back at Marcy's house. sitting around in our pajamas, raiding the refrigerator, giggling and happy. When I look back on that night, it seems like no big deal—such a harmless typical American eighth grade evening. But it was a great gift from the Wensleys and marked one of the high points of my relationship with them. I thought it was the grandest evening of my life so far.

Exploding—Like Pollen in July

DURING THE SUMMER before my freshman year, Marcy and I went out for cheerleading. The day before we were supposed to try out, I slept over at her house. Cari came to pick us up at school the next day. But the tryouts had ended early, and we had already returned to Marcy's house. When she finally caught up with me, Cari was furious that she had driven all the way to Bennington from Shaftsbury and that I wasn't where I said I would be. I tried to explain, but it was no use. She thought that I had lied. And to tell her that I hadn't lied was like accusing *her* of lying and just made her madder.

We began to clash frequently. She would get mad, and I would sulk. Starting when I was in the seventh grade, Cari had been going to work more and more, leaving me in charge of the younger kids every day after school. I loved them and had never minded babysitting, feeding them dinner, putting them in the tub, getting them to bed. But as high school approached, I was starting to get sick of it, just the way I was sick of my youth group.

Cari told me sternly that there were certain responsibilities in being part of a family. *Right! Fine!* I wanted to say. But when people always *expect* you to do something for them, it makes you really not want to do it. Only I didn't say that. I just glowered and moped. She said that I had an attitude, that I was a disrespectful girl, *that I was still exactly the same way I had been when I came to live with them!*

There it was. The past. No matter how much I tried to prove to my foster parents that I was not a bad little girl anymore, it was never enough. Cari would always joke about how as a kid I used to walk around with a terrible pout on my face. And ten years later, we'd have a fight and I'd get a pout on my face, and she would insist, "There. You see? She hasn't changed."

It was as though they had forgotten how lousy my life had been when I was a little girl. Instead of being sensitive to my emotions, they used my emotions against me, constantly reminding me of what an unhappy child I had been and how awful it was to have an unhappy person around the house. It drove me nuts! Every time they would get angry at me, it would be as though we were back at Day One. I said to myself it was because they had never really forgotten that I wasn't theirs and that I was still a guest in their home and always would be.

Our adoption worker was bringing over all kinds of stuff for Cari to read to explain my changing state of mind—articles with titles like "Adopting the Abused Child," "Love Is Not Enough," and "Mood Disorders in Young People." Judging from the reading list, Cari must have felt she had a real problem.

I know I sure did.

Stepping Out With Marcy

MY FRESHMAN YEAR in high school was the high point of my life so far. Now that Marcy was my best friend, I didn't have to be a tagalong any more. I was happy. Popular. Comfortable. Marcy helped me secure a job at the ice cream stand where she worked, and I babysat, and it was so great because I always had money in my pocket!

One of the star soccer players got a crush on me and asked me out. I said I would go if Marcy could come along. Can you imagine? I was so nervous about dating that I had to have my guardian around at all times.

"Please come," I pleaded.

"What are you, crazy?"

"Just come along with us."

"You're too old for a chaperon, Charlotte."

"What if he tries to kiss me?"

"You'll live through it. Trust me."

So we went to his house and watched a movie. He wanted to make out. I didn't want to. So he stopped seeing me. I couldn't have cared less. I didn't want to be with someone who just liked me for my looks. I wanted someone who thought I had a mind, someone I could talk to, who would give me support. Then, weeks later, when we were at a party and lots of guys were paying attention to me, this soccer player started getting jealous and liking me again. I began to realize that guys in high school are just like girls. Mostly all they care about is what their friends think of them and not how things are but how they *look* to everybody else.

After the soccer player, I dated a hippie. At least that's what I think he was. He had long hair and an earring and could usually be found sitting by himself in the bleachers that ringed the athletic fields, playing the saxophone or reading some book that looked hard. His eccentricity, his independent, carefree attitude fascinated me. I remember having a crush on him but being afraid to say anything. And then this girl Cocoa—who later became my worst enemy—called me up and said he wanted to take me to the homecoming dance.

We had a blast.

I was fourteen years old. I had the attention span of a sitcom watcher. The most important thing I could think of to do was to meet my friends at a dance club called Alfie's. I sat down and tried to talk to Cari and Bill about my feelings, how I really wanted to go to this place.

"It's a bar, Charlotte!"

"Well, okay, yes, it's a bar, but on Thursday nights, obviously, because it's kids' night, they don't have liquor. They have soda."

"I don't know . . ."

"Please, Mom. Please."

Somehow, I got through to Cari.

She made up a contract. Just like that. I could go out every night if I wanted to, as long as I maintained a C average. The whole plan seemed really sketchy and completely out of character for Cari. But I wasn't going to question it.

She told Diana I'd blow it for sure.

And to her mind, I did. I went to Alfie's every Thursday and hung out with Marcy after school almost every day. I got warnings in a couple of subjects and fell below C in math.

So the Wensleys took it all away. All of it. They didn't say, "This is what we think you can handle—a movie on Friday, a dance on Saturday." They took it *all* away. They said I would have to stay home weekends until I was doing better in school.

I steamed and stewed and suffocated in my basement room and became angrier and angrier as time went by. I felt so cheated. Why couldn't I have the friends I wanted? I wasn't hanging around with juvenile delinquents or anything! Just because my friends weren't fundamentalist Protestants didn't mean they came from bad families! Why couldn't I live like a normal kid in the real world?! Why were my feelings being ignored and disrespected? I fell into one of my old conversations with myself. *I don't need them. I can leave here. Any time I want. I can move in with Marcy and her mother. Or somebody.*

The Last Round in Shaftsbury

ONE DAY CARI announced she was coming to school to clean out my locker. She told Diana that in this way she hoped to make me reconsider my "disrespectful" attitude. I said I could clean my locker myself. She said she would come to school with me and watch me do it.

The problem was that there were swear words written all over my locker: stupid immature profane graffiti that just collected on the lockers over the years, kind of like the prehistoric wall paintings in those caves in France. Only these wall paintings said things like "Welcome to the Fuck Factory," and I knew Cari would freak out if she saw that, and nothing would convince her that I had not written it. So I called Marcy.

"You've got to help me! She's coming to school! She'll see!"

Marcy covered up all the graffiti with whatever she could find, like army posters and bumper stickers from music festivals.

Cari and I drove to school and she made happy small talk, but I was so angry when I got out of the car, I slipped on the ice and went flying. She asked me if I was okay. I was sure she was really laughing at me. She stood by me and watched me clean out my locker—in front of everybody. I was so humiliated, I wanted to melt!

After that, Cari and Bill decided the school itself was corrupting my morals and thought maybe Cari should teach me at home. She had several friends who were home-schooling their children—a trend among some folks in our area who, for example, wanted to teach creationism instead of evolution and found the public schools unwilling to do it for them.

The threat of home schooling made me totally hysterical!

School was everything to me! Freedom! Privacy! Growth!

But to my foster parents, it seemed to be the fountain of my rebellion.

I wanted to say, "Don't you get it? The reason I'm being so rebellious is that you're not communicating with me, not listening to me, not letting me be my own person! I'm not like you. I'm totally different; I come from a totally different culture than you do. *How can you expect me to be just like you?*"

I *wanted* to say that, but I couldn't.

I pouted, I glared, I moped, but I never said what was in my heart. The old "I don't need you" thing crept over me like a glacier. Soon I was as frozen as the quarry lake in winter.

ONE DAY MARCY and I went to the Blue Benn Diner to have breakfast. We were late for school and missed first period, so we received in-school suspension. That's where you sit in a room all day long and do nothing. It was one of those big unforgivable sins at the Wensleys, because it had the extra ingredient of publicity. *Other people* now thought I was a bad kid: the teachers, the principal. The Wensleys felt that hurt the reputation of our family. They were so mad, they grounded me for a month. I could go to school, but then I had to come straight home and stay in my room. They didn't lock the door, but they told me I absolutely could not come out for anything except to go to the bathroom. I had to eat in there, and nobody could visit me— not Laura, not Billy, not Diana, not my friends, nobody.

That's about the point at which my rebellion ceased to be a bunch of coming attractions and took on feature-presentation status. I couldn't believe that this was the punishment for having breakfast at the diner and getting in-school suspension! Big deal! And besides, I thought I was too old for this kind of punishment! I was in high school, and here they were, doing the same thing to me that they had done to Diana in grade school. How could parents be so mean and foolish? They took my stereo, my magazines and novels, all the stuff I liked. They left my school books and my Bible and that was all. Toward the end of my grounding, they let me come out to eat dinner, but then I had to go back to my room.

And they didn't *talk* to me about it—that was the worst thing. They were just so mad that they fell into a rigid silence. The old terror of rejection crept over me again. I shivered from the cold of it. *They're going to throw you out, Charlotte. You're a bad little girl. You've done something wrong. They don't love you. Out you go.* But I knew myself by now. I knew that I had to overcome my own fear and strike out for myself.

I started sneaking out.

Diana knew, and she helped me.

I had sneaked out to parties before and had a couple of beers, but now I started trying to get more seriously drunk on beer and liquor. Instead of just experimenting with a few puffs of marijuana, I started trying to get really high.

This was "having a good time," I told myself.

But inside, I was aching.

MY BASEMENT ROOM opened onto the area where we kept the toys and the TV. Bill's workshop also opened onto this area. So did the garage. The door to my room was only fifteen feet or so from a door that led outside. Even if somebody was watching

TV, they couldn't see the door to my bedroom, which was behind the TV area and around a little corner. If I was really quiet, and the TV show was really interesting, I could tiptoe from my bedroom door out the back door and nobody would notice. I managed to do that one time when Bill was watching TV, and he didn't catch me. I didn't have to worry that they were going to come in and say "Good night, Charlotte" and discover my absence, because the whole point of being isolated in your room was that nobody came in to say anything.

I'd go to school during the day, and Marcy and I would plan a place and a time, or sometimes I could sneak to a phone in my house to call her. I'd say, "I'll be down at the end of the road at such and such a time, and I'll wait fifteen minutes, and if you're not there, I'll go home." That night, I would wait for the right moment and sneak out. I'd leave something in the back door to keep it ajar so I could get back in, or I'd get back in through the garage door or the bathroom window—which were both usually open, since people don't fear crime in little Vermont towns as much as they do in big cities.

On one night, I remember, there was a big party that I really wanted to go to. I had arranged to meet Marcy as usual. But I couldn't get out! Bill was working on something in his workshop. Back and forth he would go from the shop to the basement, from the shop to the basement, while the rest of the family watched TV.

I didn't know what to do.

I was trapped.

So I pretended I was the cat.

"*Meow,*" I said. "*Meow. MEOW!*"

I pretended to open the door to let out the cat, and I ran outside. I was gone when Bill returned from his shop, but he didn't know it, and the family was still sitting in front of the TV set.

Because I had fooled the Wensleys a couple of times, I thought I could fool them forever. So I got lazy. Instead of making arrangements at school, I wrote a note to my friends and had no idea—until I read my case file—that Bill and Cari had intercepted it.

One night, I heard there was going to be a big party up at the winter camp of one of the kids. I stuffed my bed with pillows and took the porcelain doll that Grammy had given me and put her under the covers and spread out her brown hair on the pillow as if it were mine. I put on my big waterproof boots and two layers of sweatshirts and my hat and my mittens and slipped out.

The camp was out in the woods, one of those places that Vermont people keep to hole up in during the winter when they're hunting or fishing. Basically it's a cabin with some food and lots of booze. We all got into some guy's little sports car, and he drove off the road into the woods. The trouble was that it was snowing really hard. We couldn't see anything. We were laughing and having this great time, but basically we had not one clue where we were going, and when we got to the camp in one piece, it was like a total miracle.

It was freezing. We had to light a fire. All they had there was hard liquor: vodka, gin, rum, schnapps of all kinds. I just drank. And when I was finished drinking, I shared a bottle of champagne with one kid. I threw up. It was awful. But the kids were nice. It made me feel good, because I was getting attention. If I had to throw up in the snow to get it, so be it. Still, deep inside I knew I didn't want this to be the kind of good time that made me happy.

I sobered up by one o'clock and got home by two o'clock in the morning.

The basement door was locked. The garage door was locked. And the bathroom window was locked. Near the back deck, I found two bean bag chairs that were being thrown out, so I snuggled down between them, and with the heavy clothes I was wearing and the residual alcohol still heating up my insides, I was really warm, and I fell asleep.

I slept until four o'clock, when I woke up to realize that Cari and Bill were dragging me into the house and dumping me on my bed. They said they knew all along that I had been sneaking out, that with all my drinking and pot-smoking and messing around with guys, *I was turning out just like my mother.*

I wanted to scream: "No, no, that is not true! You do not get the picture! I am not a drunk! I am not a junkie! I am not a whore! I am doing this to get your attention! Because you are not listening to me, not responding to my needs!"

But I didn't scream.

Even at this the most terrible moment of our lives together, I was still too scared to raise my voice to the Wensleys.

They told me that if I was going to live in their house, I would have to abide by the rules of their house. They asked me whether I would agree to that.

I said, "No."

They asked me whether I wanted to leave.

I said, "Yes."

THEY DIDN'T TRY to stop me. At eight in the morning they called SRS, who set me up with a temporary foster home.

Diana knew I had been caught. When she left that morning for her basketball tournament, she was scared something was going to happen. She called about eight-thirty. I told her I was moving. She started crying.

"I don't want you to leave!"

"Stop crying. It's over. I'm out of here."

We had always been together. We had always relied on each

other. And now it was blowing up in our faces. My poor sister was sobbing, but I was so angry and sick of everything at that moment that I did not shed one tear.

"Where can I call you?" she cried.

"I don't know. I have no idea where they are going to send me. But I'll write to you, Diana. I'll call you."

I had to get my things together. I had a wet pile of wash in the washing machine and asked if I could put it in the dryer. Cari said no. She gave me another garbage bag for my wet clothes. So there I was, on my way to the next stopover, a ward of the state with her belongings in two garbage bags.

Bill didn't come in the car with us that morning. It was just Cari and me. She took me to the house of a nice woman, brought my plastic bags into the house, and said goodbye. She didn't hug me. Nothing. She just left. I didn't see her again for months.

I ask myself over and over how things between me and the Wensleys got so bad. Whatever the answers may be, they center on the fact that I was not adopted, and I could never forget that. I got there when I was three and left when I was fourteen—almost eleven years—and in all that time, these words had never been said: "We are making a full, legal commitment to you. We are adopting you. We are your family."

It took a tremendous toll.

I loved the Wensleys but still I didn't feel close to them, because I was scared of them and didn't feel confident that I could tell them the truth of my heart. I felt that I could never get the emotional support that I needed there, and I never bonded. That's why I left so easily and never went back.

CHAPTER *F*OUR

WHEN YOU LOSE your family, and you know that nobody is
thinking about your future except yourself, you start looking
for a treasure. Too bad it can't be an easy-to-capture play treasure, like the beads and pebbles and barrettes that Diana and
Billy and I fought for when we were little kids. Looking for a
real treasure is much more exhausting and depressing. For me,
it took the shape of a college education.

How can I get an education so I can get a job? I asked myself.
*How can I get an education so I can get a job and pay rent and
feed myself? How can I get a college education so that I can get
a job and support myself and get married and support my children, so that being family-less will not be a horrible financial
burden my whole life through?*

These are the questions that a girl in foster care asks herself.
So imagine how this girl felt when she read the list of prizes that
they were giving to the lucky young woman who would win the
1993 Miss Teen USA Pageant:

> $30,000 from her employment contract with Miss Uni-
> verse, Inc.
> $5,000 cash awarded by the Miss Teen USA College Schol-
> arship Fund to assist in expenses for her college of choice

$7,500 cash and a one-year supply of cosmetics from Cover Girl

$7,500 cash plus $500 in vision care for the whole family from the Contact Lens Council

$7,500 cash plus a supply of Precisely Right home permanent products from Ogilvie

$7,500 cash plus an assortment of Cosmetic Organizers in hot styles and colors from Caboodles

$7,500 cash plus a year's supply of Arrid Teen Image antiperspirant from Carter-Wallace

$5,000 cash plus a $3,000 wardrobe of the latest in sportswear and swimwear fashions from Catalina

A 1994 Pontiac Sunbird Convertible Coupe including air, stereo cassette, rear speaker, power windows, and choice of six colors, awarded by Pontiac Division of General Motors Corporation

A two-year college scholarship offering an AA Degree in Fashion Merchandising, Interior Design or Fashion Design, $15,000 total value from Bauder College, Atlanta, Georgia

A $12,000 shopping spree at Flemington's, offering her choice of leather and fur coats and jackets, awarded by Flemington Fur Company

A complete 35mm Minolta Maxxum SLR camera outfit, a master camcorder, autofocus binoculars, Weathermatic camera kit, Minolta fax machine, and more, totaling $8,000, from Minolta Corp.

A seven-day Caribbean cruise for four from Carnival Cruise Line

A one-week vacation in Hawaii for two (or $2,000 cash) plus a year's supply of sun-care products from Hawaiian Tropic

A $3,000 collection of elegant Frederico-Leone footwear
from Colonial Shoe Company, Atlanta, Georgia
A $5,000 personal appearance travel wardrobe including
luggage from Miss Universe, Inc.

Not to mention the crown and the trophy.

When I dared to think about that list of prizes, I didn't imagine them as the rewards for winning a contest. To me, they were the key to the future I wanted desperately, a future I was sure I had cut myself off from the day I entered the home of Janet Henry on Silver Street in Bennington, Vermont.

That I found such a treasure in this day and age, from the limbo of foster care—that was the miracle of my life.

The House on Silver Street

JANET HENRY IS a round, redheaded woman with a big heart and what they call a "checkered history," which she herself will be happy to tell you all about. At any given time, she is natural mother to four of her own children and foster mother to six to ten of everybody else's. Her big old house on Silver Street in Bennington serves as safe haven for wayward, desperate, lost, victimized, screwed-up kids. Seventeen rooms. A sagging front porch carpeted by electric-green Astroturf. A big kitchen. Eight bedrooms, as spare and clean as little churches, except for all the teddy bears and floppy-legged dolls that sit propped up against the pillows. Janet takes in survivors of crimes, potheads, dropouts, runaways, kids who have been so abused by the adults who were supposed to care for them that they are in a perpetual state of nervous crisis and can barely hold a conversation or eat a meal or make a friend.

Most kids land in foster care because of reasons beyond their control: Somebody died, or somebody went crazy and became incompetent, or somebody got sick and had to go to the hospital, or there was a financial disaster or a divorce, in which all the responsible adults just fell to pieces. But the great majority of people don't realize that. They think that all foster kids are juvenile delinquents. Mention the fact that you're a foster child, and many folks assume you spend your days shoplifting at Penney's.

We did have thieves at Janet's house. But most of them were just trying to get attention. Other kids were just regular old CHINS: Children in Need of Supervision, who, as our former social worker Catherine Cadieux puts it, had "blown out of their homes." Like me.

On one side of Janet's house were the group foster home facilities—the living rooms, the kitchen, and some of the bedrooms. On the other side was what SRS called the "independent living" quarters, where responsible kids who were old enough could live on their own, with fewer rules and a little more privacy.

The front steps, the floors, the pictures on the walls, the pathway from the foster care side to the independent living side—all of these pieces of Janet's house were kind of lopsided and bent out of shape, just like us kids who lived there. The main wall in the living room was covered with pictures of us. Almost two hundred children in thirteen years. And in the two and a half years that I spent with Janet, I lived with fifty-three of them.

Janet will tell you that she was fifteen when she got pregnant and sixteen when she ran away from home. She had divorces, had more kids, worked at all kinds of jobs (including go-go dancer), and ended up on welfare. That was when SRS discovered her talent for taking care of troubled children. They encouraged her to make a career of it and helped her turn her life around. In 1988, Janet received her BS in Human Services and Criminal Justice and was licensed to run a foster home. In 1992, she was voted Foster Mother of the Year in Vermont.

"I was a runaway," Janet says, "which is why I relate so well to these scared adolescents, physically and sexually abused children, unwed mothers. I know how bad the alcohol and drug abuse is, because I did it. When the kids come home, I can smell their clothes and tell them what kind of pot they were smoking. I have been through a lot of terrible things in my life. And I understand what these kids go through and I want my home to be a haven for them."

I CAME TO her on February 11, 1991. She took a look at my "record"—sneaking out at night, drinking, smoking pot, and (according to some guy who told it to Cari who told it to our social worker, who noted it in my case files as if it were the Truth) using LSD and cocaine too—not to mention the sex everybody thought I was having, even though I totally wasn't—and she figured I was a bad seed. She took me to a room and showed me what to do with the garbage bags that contained my few possessions. I had left the Wensleys so fast that I forgotten some pretty important things: all my pictures, my diaries, sacred memorabilia that I would never be able to retrieve. On a more practical level, Marcy had to bring me a couple of bras.

Janet called my attention to the twenty-eight ironclad house rules, which were posted on the kitchen wall. I would get a thirty-day trial period to see if I was going to stay or go back to Bill and Cari or if some other family would take me in. I couldn't make any phone calls until a few days into the orientation week. I would have to cooperate and fit in with the six other teenage kids—all older than I was—who currently lived here. The curfew was at ten o'clock, eleven o'clock on the weekends. Except for school, I couldn't be out of the house for more than three hours at a time. I could watch a television show if I applied to watch it beforehand and if nobody else had applied before me to watch something else in that time slot. No drugs. No alcohol. No smoking. No sex in the house. No dirty talk. No fighting. If you failed a subject, you were grounded. If you stole something, you had to give it back and you were grounded. And on and on and on.

Once I heard a character on an episode of the television show *Law and Order* say that a group foster home is "no better than a prison." When I saw Janet Henry's twenty-eight house rules, I felt just that way.

The Rules at Janet Henry's House

1. *All issues will be honestly and openly discussed. Therefore, lies will result in loss of night or nights out.*
2. *Stealing will not be tolerated. The issue will be discussed and dealt with on an individual basis. Inventory will be taken on arrival and when you leave.*
3. *Articles which are not your own personal possessions are not to be taken from this house.*
4. *When I am not home, no one is allowed to enter the house except those who live here. Permission must be given by me for friends to come and visit. Visits during evening hours will be limited. Exception: All SRS social workers.*
5. *No drugs and alcohol in or around the house. I will keep and dispense all medication.*
6. *Anyone who comes home stoned or drunk will be grounded for one month.*

Diana and me at two and three years old—the earliest picture that I have of us

Diana and me, five and six years old, at Easter

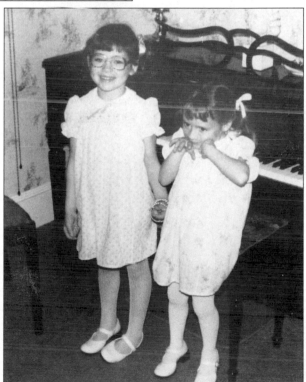

Three years old, at the carnival

My first grade-school picture

My second-grade picture

My sister and me, with a friend, camping in Maine

Six-year-old Diana hamming it up for the camera

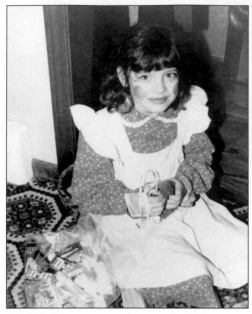

Halloween at the Wensleys'. I was Raggedy Ann.

My first modeling picture. I was nine years old.

Janet Henry's house on Silver Street

Christmas portrait with me and other foster kids at Janet Henry's group home

For fun, I had this picture taken during my junior year. I was sixteen.

Taking goofy pictures with my roommate at Janet Henry's group home during my second year there (1992)

Me in my friends' Odyssey after a day in the woods (high school)

Christmas at Janet's

At the Miss Vermont Teen USA Pageant

Diana and I putting on one of our many performances

Spending precious time with my sister, Diana, waterskiing in New Jersey

At a charity auctioning off a Vermont Baby Black Bear

With my good friends Alicia, Susie, January, and Jill at the pageant

Singing my heart out at karaoke with friends and fellow contestants Miss Maine, Miss Massachusetts, and Miss Colorado

Living it up at a pageant gala

The interview with Dick Clark

*The swimsuit
competition.
I came in third.*

Down to the six-semifinalists

Proudly representing my state in the evening gown competition, with my $37 gown. (I was second overall.)

Standing before the judges for the final vote

Being crowned by fellow titleholders: Miss USA, Miss Teen USA, and Miss Universe

Almost fainting with happiness in my new throne

Signing my first autographs

With Janet after the contest

With Judge Sally Cook, Al, Jill, and Diana at my adoption, March 7, 1994, at the Manchester Court House

On the phone in a hotel talking to my parents after the pageant

With Senator Jim Jeffords

With Diane Sawyer at my home in Vermont

With Janet Reno at CASA Conference in Tampa, Florida

At a luncheon with fellow foster kids

Me holding an adorable foster baby

Me in May 1994, relaxing before a big speaking engagement

My sister and best friend, Diana

Me at home in Dorset, Vermont

7. *No long distance calls unless permission is given and arrangements have been made to pay for the call(s).*

8. *No incoming or outgoing calls before 9:00 A.M. or after 9:00 P.M. No fighting or arguing allowed on the phone. Timer must be set for ten minutes. Permission to use the phone from me or supervisor.*

9. *Respect to all members of the household is necessary for a happy and harmonious home; therefore, all complaints must be discussed and worked out through a family meeting whenever someone feels it is necessary.*

10. *Nights out require two days previous notice. During the week (Sun through Thurs) age 14 and up, 10:00 P.M. curfew. Weekends (Fri and Sat) one night, 11:00 curfew. Under 14s worked out individually.*

11. *Lateness will be dealt with according to: time, reason, condition you come home in, and frequency of lateness. Grounding could result.*

12. *Everyone is expected to be home for the dinner hour (5:30 to 6:30 P.M.) unless special arrangements have been made. Kitchen is closed at 7:00 P.M.*

13. *Grades must be maintained at a reasonable level (C). Any failures or drops in grades will result in fewer nights out. Improvements in all grades will be rewarded with an extra night out every other week of your choice. Any A's received will be rewarded with $3, any B's with $1.*

14. *Bedtime is 10:00 P.M. Sun through Thurs. Lights out is at your discretion. If you are sharing a room it becomes a mutual agreement. If an agreement cannot be reached, I will help. TV must be off at 10:00 P.M. No all-night radios upstairs after 9:00 P.M.*

15. *I am always available to talk, if you need help or just want to talk. This home is open to all subjects of discussion.*

16. *Unless you display behavior which is inappropriate, you will be treated as a responsible young adult. (This means controlling yourself in public places or you will not be in public places!)*

17. *No form of verbal or physical abuse will be tolerated in this home. Anger of any form will be discussed in a civil manner with respect given for all feelings involved. We tend to say things we do not mean in anger and hurt the feelings of others.*

18. *You are expected to keep your room clean and neat. The bed must be made every day. There will be no exceptions. $5 fine for violations.*

19. *Smoking is not allowed in the house under any condition. Anyone found smoking will lose one week out.*

20. *All therapy sessions must be attended.*

21. *Cutting school is not allowed. I will allow occasional days off based on grades and general behavior both inside and outside the house.*

22. *Everyone (except Mom) will take turns doing the two chores (dishes and vacuuming).*

23. *You are expected to clean up after yourself. We are all too busy to clean someone else's mess.*

24. *Due to problems which have arisen, wearing articles of clothing or shoes which are not your own is not permitted. If your clothing allowance is spent wisely, in time you will have plenty of clothes. If clothing is not appropriate, you may not wear it! I determine that.*

25. *No swearing in or around this house. Swearing will result in 1/2 hour off your next night out.*

26. *Drive-in movies, rock concerts, amusement parks, malls, out-of-town day trips: age 17 and up. Exceptions can be made at my discretion for all ages.*

27. *You will consistently and correctly report your where-abouts at all times.*
28. *Seven-day orientation for all incomers.*
Grounding: Loss of all privileges, expected to be home within 1/2 hour after leaving school. Exception—job. No phone calls in or out.

These rules of Janet Henry's were famous in the small foster care community of southern Vermont.

"We knew that our rules were like paradise in comparison," Cari said in an interview with *Glamour*. Bill said they thought sending me to Janet was an act of "tough love," that I would surely "hate it and come home."

Our Lovable Warden

THE KEY TO Janet's ability to discipline kids isn't force. It's common sense, moral authority, and a sense of humor. She's not tall; she's not muscular; she wouldn't raise her hand to smack any kid. But I've seen her psyche out and intimidate some giant, mean guys so that they actually came around and did what she wanted. She just wasn't afraid of the kids. She identified with them. When nobody else could handle them, she could some-how.

For instance, there was Hank, who was over six feet, with muscles of steel and nerves of yogurt. He was down on Main Street, high on drugs and causing a disturbance. Since he resisted arrest, the cops put him in the lockup first. Then, when he calmed down, they brought him over to Janet's.

When Janet told him to sit down and listen to the house rules, describing to him how he was going to have to make beds and wash dishes, he flew into such a wild rage that he put his fist through the living room wall.

"Ah, well, so much for the wall. I always hated that wall anyway."

"You fat bitch!"

"I say we pick up some paint and plaster and repair it tomorrow."

"Fuck you! Fuck you! Fuck you!"

"You wanna help pick out the colors?"

"Aghhhh!"

"No, huh? Well then, Hank, I guess you're going to have to go to juvenile jail."

So the cops came and off went Hank to the lockup. After a few days, he called.

"Janet? Can I come home? I promise I'll fix the wall, I'll do the dishes . . ."

During my first several months at Janet's house, I was grounded a few times until I learned the routine. For example, I didn't have any money, so Diana gave me $15. I bought deodorant, shampoo, and a pair of $6 pants. Janet took the pants away because I couldn't show her the receipt, which I had thrown away. If you came home with a new item, you had to show the receipt to prove that you had not stolen it. She wasn't accusing me of stealing, she said. It was just that so many other kids in the house stole all the time that receipt-showing was house policy. Those were the rules. Still, I felt that because of what the Wensleys had told her about me, Janet really thought I had stolen them.

Feeling hysterical because I could never be out for longer than three hours at a time, I would lie about my whereabouts. Feeling trapped because I could never do anything spontaneously—like go to a movie or a party—I would just bolt and run and say I was at athletic practice or something. Janet would come looking for me and she would always find out that I wasn't where I had said I would be—and I would get grounded. My boss remembers that I used to ask her to stand watch for Janet's car as she came cruising down the street, looking to see if I was really there. When Janet found out that I wasn't—and she invariably did—I would be grounded.

I thought of myself as a lonely, frustrated, confused teenager who wanted someone to listen to her and respect her for who she was. But people in church, at SRS—even my little brother Billy and his friends and my little sister Laura—believed that I was a wild, boozing, drugged-out, disrespectful, promiscuous liar. At our congregation, prayers were being said for me. When I would pass somebody from the church, they would look at me with such pity, like, "Oh poor child, the devil has possessed her! That curse her mother put on her years ago has really come true!"

Why bother being cooperative when everybody in town has been told you're the devil's spawn? I guess I figured that obviously they put me in this place with all these juvenile delinquents because they think I'm like them.

Well, maybe I am.

Hell, maybe I *will* be.

It is so easy to fulfill low expectations!

The one person in Bennington who seemed *not* to believe everything she had heard about me was Janet Henry. There was something lighter about the way Janet took all my teenage bullshit. She didn't think I was the spawn of Satan because I lied to her about where I was. She could put things in perspective. She knew I was not a juvenile delinquent! For God's sakes, she had kids in her house who were robbing convenience stores and getting pregnant at fourteen! Compared with them, I was Mother Teresa!

One night soon after I arrived, I was sitting at the little desk in the front room, doing my homework. Janet approached me.

"Charlotte, can I talk to you about something?"

"Sure. What?"

"Well, Charlotte, whenever a new girl comes in and they're going out with guys . . . well . . . I want you to know that I have protection for you right here."

She opened the drawer of the little desk and showed me this big pile of condoms. I just sort of stared at them.

"Have you had a Pap smear yet?" she asked.

"What uh no uh . . ."

"You should really think about going on the pill, maybe getting a diaphragm, and you have to use condoms all the time to protect yourself from AIDS. And we should make an appointment for you to go to your family doctor, or maybe Planned Parenthood."

"For what?"

"For birth control!"

"Don't you have to have sex to need birth control?"

Jane took a deep breath and said, "You know what, Charlotte? Forget it. Forget I ever mentioned anything about it. You don't have to go to the doctor." Then, as she recalls, Janet went into her room and closed the door and called the social worker and hollered, *"Oh my God! I've got a virgin! What do I do now?"*

Transition Time

IT WAS VERY hard for me to readjust in school after I left the Wensleys. Everybody seemed to have heard some version of the story of our breakup. I had suddenly been transformed from a girl with a home and a family to a rejected outcast, living on the public dole, in the next thing to a prison. All my legitimacy evaporated. I changed my name back to Lopez. My friends needed permission to visit me. I couldn't come or go in freedom. Every move I made was timed and recorded.

I felt so lost, so robbed of my dignity that I thought I would lose my mind. I threw myself into academic work just to think about something besides who might still love me in this world. By the middle of April, my grades were A in math and gym and B in science, social studies, and English. (I also scored a big fat D-minus failure in French. So much for that "French blood" Emma bragged about.) Janet reported to the new social worker that I wasn't doing drugs or drinking.

The new social worker, Angela, was tough and attentive and lots of fun. For all the years that I had been a "good girl," SRS almost never spoke to me. Now that I had been labeled a "bad girl," SRS occupied a much more obvious presence in my life. Angela drove a lumbering Chrysler and never hesitated to pop over and give me hell if I got out of line.

She and I had long discussions about the Wensleys. Did I want to go back? Did I want to meet with them? Talk with them? Work it out so things could be civil and comfortable between us? Truthfully, I just didn't know. I'd change my mind from one day to the next. Angela recalls that I "had a lot of anger." She was astonished at my firmly held belief that I had not been adopted because SRS had lost the adoption papers.

It made me burn to hear that my family was taking a vacation to help themselves recover from the trauma of my departure, while I was settling into a foster home where almost everything I owned was being swiped by some sick kleptomaniac and I had roommates who screamed in their sleep. I depended on Marcy and her family for contact with the outside world, for comfort and kind words. Although Marcy didn't like to visit me at Janet's, I ran over to her house every chance I got.

Lydia, our adoption worker, suggested mediation to the Wensleys. The case files say they were agreeable as long as I "fully accepted the need" for mediation as well. Truthfully, I don't recall Lydia ever bringing it up to me. The minister of our church came around to see me, but he didn't mention reconciliation. My feeling was that my old family was just enormously relieved to have me out of their house, relieved not to have to deal with a difficult adolescent anymore, glad that I could no longer "corrupt" their other children.

What's more, I was fifteen and inclined to be on the dramatic side. Forgive and forget wasn't enough for me. I imagined a grand, melodramatic reunion, when I would apologize and be apologized to. I wanted the Wensleys to swallow their pride and be ready to talk about their mistakes as well as mine. It was a teenage fantasy. It never happened.

The Wensleys had their own point of view.

"We thought SRS would be there to help us," Bill told *Glamour*. "But there was no discussion with us, and we were told Charlotte had no interest in returning."

"We thought it would be a short-term thing," Cari said, "that Charlotte would learn some lessons. But after she left, no one was there to stand up for us as parents. Charlotte's decision not to return broke our hearts."

BENNINGTON, VERMONT, IS a smallish town with a famous college, a lovely museum, a couple of really sophisticated bookstores, some good restaurants, a big gun-and-ammunitions market, and a lot of wonderful old clapboard houses with painted trim. In the winter, the whole place looks like the label on a maple syrup tin. People put up nice Christmas decorations and often don't take them down until the Big Melt, which typically doesn't come until March.

As far as I was concerned, Bennington was the center of the world. I had never lived in a town before and found it a great new experience. Instead of riding over the mountains under a black and starry sky in some guy's Land Rover, looking for a place to hang out that wasn't the Land Rover itself, I could just mosey into the center of town and hang with my friends on Main Street and window-shop in the chic little stores.

I had become what foster kids usually are—officially and literally poor, receiving from the state my room and board and health care and $60 a month ($45 for clothes and $15 for personal items like haircuts and toothpaste). The little amenities of regular family life had disappeared. I now had no one to drive me to soccer practice or my appointments at SRS. I needed a bike with two good tires and money in my pocket. The job that Marcy helped me find at the local ice cream stand answered the need.

All through April, May, and June, I stood at the little window, serving up fries and dogs and ice cream. In the early evening I would ride my bike home in the shadow of Mount Anthony. People would wave to me because they knew me now—I was "Charlotte from Janet Henry's house."

Things were getting ever so slightly better for me. But one thing was getting worse, and that was my precious friendship with Marcy.

She wanted to party—and I couldn't get out at night.

She was still smoking pot, and I didn't dare.

First of all, I knew that Janet would smell it on me and ground me yet again. And second, if I ever needed proof that doing drugs would surely screw my whole life totally, it swirled around me like a hurricane at Janet's house, where some of the kids were so spaced out that they couldn't remember who they had slept with or what they had stolen the night before.

I was pulling away from the hard-core party crowd that I had wanted so desperately to join only a year earlier. Marcy must have felt really hurt by that. Her friend Cocoa, who had always been jealous of our relationship, was right on hand to say, "I told you so. Charlotte Lopez is basically an uptight church mouse and a big snob." And her friend Pat, a beautiful redhead whose insecurities outdistanced even mine, decided it was time to push me out of the picture entirely.

In June, Marcy and one of her other friends told my bosses at the ice cream stand that I was drinking and doing drugs before coming to work, and that I would be stoned on the job. And because the bosses knew them better than me, they believed them.

"We trusted you, Charlotte, and now this!" my boss said over the phone.

"But it's not true! You're just listening to gossip! I would never think of coming to work stoned or buzzed! This job is too important to me, and I'm not stupid!"

My boss just hung up. I was crying hysterically.

Janet tried to comfort me. But what could she say, really? It was my first job. I loved it—not just for the money but for the place in the community, the laughs, the good company. And then suddenly, whammo: out the door! My best friend had completely turned against me and had lied to get me in trouble.

It was déjà vu.

Fooled you again, Charlotte. You thought we liked you and wanted you around, but we didn't mean it. Just like all your other relationships, this one turned out to be a big bust.

I felt so abandoned! Luckily for me, one of the things I had learned at the Wensleys was to have faith in the Lord. Even though I didn't share all their religious views, I still kept my faith. Without His comfort, I wouldn't have made it through.

SRS helped me find another job, through the Bennington Boys' and Girls' Program. I supervised the little kids at the municipal camp from eight A.M. until two-thirty, then I walked over to another park and did sports with the bigger ones until four-thirty. I became friendly with the other supervisors and counselors and soon looked forward to going to work. By the time my bike rolled into Janet's driveway, I was knocked out. Exhaustion provided a kind of refuge for me. So did my anger with my old bosses—anger that they hadn't asked me but had just accused me, that they hadn't doubted the slander but rather had just believed it. Being angry and tired together is sometimes a real help. It gets you through the day.

In July, the Wensleys invited me for a cookout at what had once been my home. I was hesitant, but I went, and things were awkward but okay. After that, we got together for a couple more special occasions. They sent me postcards from their vacation and brought me back some souvenir candy. Cari brought me a present on my birthday in September. I was delighted about that. I didn't want to be mad at the Wensleys and didn't want them to be mad at me, especially since Diana, Laura, and Billy were in their house. I needed to see them and to know that they still loved me.

However, the move toward mediation just never happened. Maybe something between us had just broken too much. And truthfully, the longer I lived at Janet's, the less inclined I was to go back. This new life I was leading—which was supposed to have frightened me into submission and repentance and inspired a desperate desire to return to my old life—was actually having the opposite effect.

I was growing stronger.

Becoming a Runner

MOUNT ANTHONY HIGH School was within walking distance of Janet's house. A big, sprawling campus surrounded by fir trees and birches, it's one of those state-of-the-art new public high schools with a great weight room and plenty of computers and ramps all over to make everything accessible to physically challenged kids.

At school, I didn't hang out with the other kids from Janet's house. We were friends at home, and Janet tried to get us to think of each other as brothers and sisters, but in public we stayed clear of each other, as though we wanted people to know that we had been thrown together by chance and that we weren't really responsible for each other.

When I entered my sophomore year at Mount Anthony, I was a very different girl from the one I had been just a year before, and I needed a new kind of extracurricular life badly. I didn't want to be aloof and cool and exclusive anymore. I wanted to join, to be a member, to be involved and engaged, and most important, to be needed. I guess there's nothing like exile to make you a patriot.

But what could I join? Where would I fit in? The old crowd that I had run with the previous winter still tempted me. I really cared about Marcy and would always be grateful for the support she and her family had given me during that awful transition time when I was moving into Janet's. But Pat and Cocoa kept me at arm's length.

I was under so much stress and tension that I thought the only way I could keep going was to do something requiring discipline and strength. I was very grateful that the Wensleys had spent the time and money to teach me how to ski. There was nothing more soothing when I was stressed than to go gliding down a smooth powdered ski slope, with the sun on my face and the snow blowing all around me. I joined the ski club at school and met new friends.

I had played soccer before in junior high, so I decided to try it again. The girls on the team were nice, and it seemed like a good way to get involved. But I was never really good at soccer.

What really engaged my energy was the track team.

The girls on the team were a whole new experience for me—jocks from good families who played because they believed that having muscles and raising a sweat was important for their health. They were nice to me. In the wintertime, I did indoor track. That's when I started weight lifting. I wanted to keep in shape. I had seen on TV how women go to the gym to lift weights and tone up. So I worked out with the football team in the weight room until my arms ached and my legs were shaking with fatigue and the sweat poured off me.

The winter track races took place inside, but the gym was booked solid, so we had to practice on the track outside. Two sweatshirts, pants over pants over tights, socks over socks—we were so bundled up, I don't know how we made it around the course. When the sweat on our eyebrows began to freeze, we would go inside and work out some more.

THE MORE I ran, the more I changed.

At the starting line, I was lost, confused, and enraged. By the finish, I was strong, confident, and secure. Running released my spirit. I ran and ran and ran away from myself and my life and my fate, and as soon as I was running and the wind was in my ears, I was okay.

Track was never about winning for me. I just loved being on a team—a needed, wanted member with a guaranteed spot in the communal effort, handing off that baton to my teammates.

They would all get upset when we lost. Not me.

All I wanted was to have a good time and get some exercise and make some friends and prove to myself that I was strong enough and fast enough to outrun this blighted destiny that life had planned for me.

One of the girls on the track team was a tall, slender brunette named Harriet. She wore her hair in one long braid. She had a long, regal nose and a gazillion freckles. She was also very smart. She got straight As, and I never once saw her crack a book. She read newspapers and played flute in the school band. In the wintertime, when the roads into school were solid ice and no bike could cross them safely, her mother would pick her up at school, and she would always offer me a lift.

We would run around the track together, paced by the sound of our sneakers hitting the frosty ground, crunch crunch, breathing clouds into the mountain air. Through Harriet, I met a new crowd—what people might call a preppy crowd. Marcy hated them. She said Harriet's crowd was snobby and upper-crust and only slumming with a girl like me. And for the longest time I believed her. But then one day Harriet invited me to have lunch with her and her friends, and they turned out to be really nice. So I had lunch with them the next day too. And the day after that. I found that far from being snobby, they were more than able to accept me and the situation I was in at Janet's house.

Janet liked Harriet much better than she liked Marcy.

I liked Harriet better than Marcy too—but guilt about that gave me butterflies in my stomach and made me sick at heart.

The Kids at Janet's House

WHEN I LOOK back on my sophomore year in high school, it seems to me that everything conspired to overturn the expectations of the people who were supposed to care for me—my foster parents, my social workers, even me—so that instead of becoming lonelier and lonelier and more and more homesick for my old family nest, I was becoming stronger and stronger and more able to fly away.

Most of the change in me was caused by my exposure to the kids at Janet's house. At first they terrified me. But after a very short while, they enthralled me. They were like a course in the great wide world that I had never been allowed to take before. Can *you* imagine living with fifty-three different people from completely different backgrounds over two and a half years? I tell you, it's the best education you can get.

We would have these marathon giant UNO games. Janet played with us. She was a big card player, but the people she liked to play with wanted to drink beer during the game, and since she wouldn't allow beer in the house she had to give up her grown-up game and get involved in UNO. We had such a fabulous time in those games! We laughed and screamed and carried on and ate chips. It was like being in a big happy club. If you won, you could get more time out, and I was always eager for more time out, so I played like a tiger and won a lot.

One night we were engrossed in our UNO game and a cop showed up at the door. We didn't pay much attention to him. We were used to cops; they came all the time, and the cop radio was often heard spitting static in our living room. But this time the cop had brought a girl, and she was in cuffs and shackles. She looked like Kevin Costner when he was playing Robin Hood in prison during the Crusades. I dropped my cards. I couldn't stop staring. She glared at me with a fury that I will never forget.

A couple of days later, she was playing UNO with us.

I went to sleep one night alone in my room and was awakened by the sound of horrible sobbing. I looked and saw that there was now another girl in the room with me. She was my age and totally hysterical.

She had just been raped.

I also lived for a while with a girl named Zeena. A bleached blonde with a two-pack-a-day cigarette habit, she had a drawer full of bizarre underwear, like a see-through net body stocking and these teeny-tiny underpants that had a flower in the front that went "Oooooh" when you pressed on it. She was a total expert on sex, and had me just about convinced that in order to have it, you really needed to own a certain nipple-less bra that you could get only from a certain emporium in Albany.

Zeena was sixteen and a pathological liar. She was totally obsessed with Jim Morrison from The Doors.

"He's alive, Charlotte. I know it. He visits me."

"Come on, Zeena, get a grip. He OD'd in Paris long ago."

"You'll see. You'll wake up in the middle of the night one night, and there he'll be, sitting on the bed . . ."

"Right. Sure."

". . . strumming his guitar and singing *Come on baby, light my fire* . . ."

So one night we went to sleep and I woke up around midnight and no, Jim Morrison was not there singing "Light My Fire." But Zeena was there, a cigarette dangling from her lips, dressed up in a sequined bra and a scarlet G-string, and stripping in the window where all the neighbors on Silver Street could see her.

I thought, *Am I dreaming this? Yes. I am definitely dreaming that Zeena is standing naked in the window.*

And I went back to sleep.

The next morning I found out it was true and Janet was shipping Zeena off for serious assistance with her mental health.

Then there was Lucy, who had run away from her home to join the carnival and then run away from the carnival to Janet's. We lived together for two days. One night I woke scratching and itching. I went to find Janet and told her that I must have picked up poison ivy; did she have any calamine lotion?

It turned out that Lucy had given me lice! Everything that she brought from the carnival was just filled with bugs. *Yuccchhh!* I washed and washed with a special shampoo, and then I washed the whole room and all the furniture and the bedding.

The thing is, Lucy may have had lice, but she was a nice person. And she straightened out in the end. She called Janet last summer and invited her to her wedding, and now she has a job and a baby and a life.

Then we had a boy named Jim. He was about twelve years old. When he came in, Janet made space for him in one of the boys' rooms. The next day he went to court with his social worker, who reported back that he absolutely refused to return to Janet's house. He hated it there, he said, and would never set foot in the place again—no way, never. Well, Janet was sort of stunned. I mean, she and Jim hadn't had any fights or anything. He seemed to be a nice enough kid. She didn't have the slightest idea why he would be unwilling to return.

Then we learned that Jim was really a twenty-three-year-old woman named Flossie, who was homeless and pretending to be a young boy so the state authorities would give her a place to stay. Only what she wanted, of course, was a single room.

Which leads me to the story of another girl I lived with: Jacqueline. She was dating this guy, and then she fell in love with his sister.

When Janet found out, Jacqueline was sure she would be thrown out of the house. But Janet would never have done that.

"I don't care if you're gay, sweetheart," she said, "as long as you don't press your sexuality on any of the girls here."

So Jacqueline stayed on. She didn't hit on any of us or anything. I continued to like her just as I always had. At the Wensleys, we were taught that homosexuality was a direct affront to

God. At Janet's, I was learning that "sin" is very often a matter of opinion. Janet was certainly not pleased that Jacqueline was gay, because she thought gay people had a hard time in life. But she certainly didn't think of Jacqueline as a sinner.

After a while, neither did I.

Learning that lesson—even being forced to think about it and come to some conclusion about it—was a perfect example of the kind of gifts that living in Janet's house brought to me. New perspectives, new philosophies, new ways of looking at the world. Somehow, the experience of rooming with all these different girls at Janet's, and hearing about all these different slices of people's lives, matured me. I gained new insight into how dangerous it was to be a foster child in this country, and how lucky I had been. I also learned how much I had to offer other people in the way of comfort and friendship—and even leadership. Because even though I was much less experienced about sex than a lot of these girls, they came to me for advice.

I tried like hell not to give too much of it.

I had learned that some of the people I was living with were so shaky and emotionally unstable that the wrong opinion from the wrong person at the wrong time could tip the scales in favor of some awful act. It was so bizarre to have these desperate girls coming into my room, sobbing and gnawing on their fingers and shaking with rage. I reacted as anybody would have. "What's the matter? Are you okay?" And then they would start pouring out their hearts to me—about unimaginable horrors, incest and beatings. They would tell me that they were going to kill themselves. At first that seemed so beyond the realm of possibility to me that I figured they were just being dramatic and making it up. But then they would try to do it! They would get up on the roof and threaten to jump. Or they would try to overdose on pills. And there I was, this good Christian from Shaftsbury, trying to make an A in history so I could get $3 more toward a big night out at Alfie's, and I was the one telling these people what to do!

Family Meetings

ONCE A WEEK without fail we had a family meeting, where everybody in the house could bring up the issues and concerns that were important to them. If there was a crisis, Janet would schedule an emergency meeting. A typical crisis was when somebody stole from somebody else, when somebody announced that they had money missing. One time this girl was caught making out with another girl's boyfriend—wow! Was *that* a crisis!

A girl named Joan came in for what Janet calls "a time-out," a month or so away from the family with which she had come to a total impasse. She had a nice house and brothers and sisters and two parents at home, but they went ballistic when she turned up pregnant. She wasn't showing much yet, but we all knew about the pregnancy.

One night at a house meeting, one of the boys asked her in a friendly way: "So, Joan. How're you feeling? When are you going to have the baby?

"Ummm . . . well . . .

"You gonna be able to take it home? You gonna give it up for adoption?"

"There is no baby," Joan said. "I'm not pregnant anymore. I had an abortion."

"WHAT?!"

A big battle started, with some of the boys attacking Joan and some of the girls defending her. I sort of mediated, and tried to remind everybody to respect each other's opinions.

Janet was happy that we were not afraid to speak up, even if that meant a fight. She wanted her kids to have the courage of their convictions. She loved the loud, strong voice of self-esteem.

I often tried to support Janet at the house meetings. There she'd be, trying to bring order and sense into our lives, and nine kids would be coming down on her, and all of them would be forgetting that because of her, they had food and a place to live and someone to talk to—that if it weren't for her, they would be sleeping in the streets!

Janet laughs about those days today. "I don't mind telling you, Charlotte was my all-time favorite," she says. "When somebody treats you good, you just like them better than someone who calls you a fat bitch. That's life."

A lot of the kids were mad at me for standing up for Janet, but I know my opinion had an impact. That meant everything to me—to have influence, to count for something. No matter how hard it was living at Janet's, I would rather have stayed there than gone back at the Wensleys'. Because at Janet's, there was total communication. Nothing was beyond discussion. Nothing. I'm a very expressive person, and I had lived with silence like a lump of poison in my throat. So it was a tremendous release for me to be in a free speech atmosphere.

I could run like the wind and lift fifty-pound weights and reconsider my personal definitions of sin.

I could be right, or totally wrong, and my opinion was respected.

I was locked up in a foster home that was supposed to be "little better than a prison," with curfews and poverty and people with problems all around, and a tough-as-nails foster mother combined with a tough-as-nails social worker who never let me get away with anything, and I had never felt so free and strong in all my life.

THE WENSLEYS INVITED me home for Christmas.

At one point, Bill and Cari and I were alone in the living room. Bill said, "We really miss you, Charlotte. You will always be part of our family. We forgive you. Would you think about it? Would you think about coming home?"

Cari just sat in the chair and looked at me.

I knew that all I had to do was to say "okay" and I could be back with the only family I had really ever known. But nearly a year had passed. And I had changed a lot—probably too much ever to return.

CHAPTER *F*IVE

IN THE MISS Teen USA Pageant, you are judged on bathing suit, evening gown, and interview. There's no talent part as there is in Miss America. But there's a lot of stage business to work out and rehearse, and that's so much fun that it distracts you from being nervous. The only thing that made me really nervous —when I had a chance to think about it—was The Interview. I worried that they would ask me about world issues I didn't understand, like Bosnia or something. I asked my roommate. She said it would be okay, not to worry. But I could see she was nervous, too.

I had one of my conversations with myself and gave myself one of my famous uplifting lectures. *Charlotte! Stop being a jerk! You have more things in your life to get nervous about than an interview! Don't look at this interview as Judgment Day. Look at it as a conversation with a reasonable, nice person.*

And that was exactly what it turned out to be.

The panel that selected Miss Teen USA 1993 was made up of reasonable, nice people: Shell Danielson and Gerald Hopkins, TV stars from the soap opera *General Hospital;* Noreen Donovan, a television producer who was responsible for the development of *Star Search* and *Lifestyles of the Rich and Famous;* Robert Harbin, vice president in charge of casting for the Fox Broadcasting Company's current programming, including *Bev-*

119

erly Hills 90210 and *In Living Color;* the hockey star Corey Hirsch; Ford model agent Anne Gorrissen; the star of *Knots Landing,* Kathleen Noone; Ernie Reyes, Jr., martial artist and actor in *Teenage Mutant Ninja Turtles II* and *Surf Ninjas;* top Hollywood producer Larry Thompson; and hot MTV VJ Kennedy Montgomery.

Each judge sat down with each contestant and held a five-minute private interview. This process took two days.

The most interesting and fun-to-answer questions for me came from Kennedy.

She asked me if I committed a crime, what would it be? If I could invest in any stock, what would it be?

I said, "I'm sixteen years old, I don't think about committing crimes and I don't keep up with the stock market, so I really have no clue what I would invest in. However, we've been studying the Depression in history class, so I can tell you about the stock market crash of 1929 if you want to hear about that."

Then she asked me when the last time was that I cried.

I told her the last time I cried was the night when I met my brother for the first time in a decade. Kennedy's eyes grew bright with interest. She leaned forward. She wanted to hear how such a thing could happen—how a person could be totally isolated from her own brother even though they lived only twenty minutes away from each other. I tried to explain to her that foster care was a very funny system, with little nooks and crannies and lots of places where people could get lost.

The Icebreaker Out in the Cold

I HAD COME to that point in my life where I couldn't go back and I didn't know which way was forward. The idea of having a family obsessed me. I still had Diana: my sister, my anchor.

But something was in the air now that had the potential to separate us.

I gather from the case files that a legal observer from SRS had been expressing concern over "why the Lopez girls haven't been adopted." His point was that because we had been available for adoption and still had not been adopted in all these years, Emma, our biological mother, could conceivably ask the court to set aside the separation of rights. And she might get us back! Obviously an adoption would save the day. Maybe that was one of the reasons that the Wensleys suddenly started talking about adopting Diana.

I tried to be really cool about that. I tried not to think, *They always loved her more than they loved you, Charlotte, and here's the proof.* I hadn't read my case files at that point, but I knew in my heart that Diana had always felt easier in our foster home, from the earliest years. She just didn't possess as keen a sense memory of being "other" as I did. When in future years we saw our natural mother on TV, I freaked out, but Diana hardly cared at all. I knew that Bill and Cari's home was the only home she had ever thought of as her own, the place where she felt committed and safe. If they also felt committed to her, then I was determined to try to put a smile on my face and be happy for everybody.

Besides, Diana reported with her usual twinkle that it was turning out to be a lot easier for her at home than it had been for me. She said that after I moved out, Bill and Cari had become more sensitive to a growing girl's need for a social life. They understood that just because you try something once or twice doesn't mean you're going to make it a lifelong habit. She said they even relaxed a little bit about religion. So there I was, feeling like the icebreaker who gets left out in the cold. What bugged me was that lack of freedom had only triggered my rebellion. It was the lack of emotional commitment that I really felt bad about. And that had never been—would probably never be—understood.

Janet wanted to adopt me. But I didn't want to be adopted by her. It wasn't that I didn't love her. I did. However, I was afraid that if I were her daughter, living in the midst of all those kids, I would be jealous of those she cared for, angry at those who gave her a hard time, and always feeling a little shortchanged.

I had come this far without being adopted, and I was doing okay. I was making Bs and Cs. That year, in indoor track, I had placed second in the state for the long jump, and I had tied for fourth in the 300-meter dash. As my second April in Janet's house rolled around, I suddenly got back my old job at the ice cream stand—no questions asked, no hard feelings. I wondered if maybe I really would be able to make it on my own without any official family.

Janet and I began to argue a lot. She felt hurt that I had turned down her offer of adoption. I felt trapped in what I considered a restrictive probationary system. None of this would have mattered at all if we hadn't cared about each other and wanted to make each other happy. I looked forward to the following September, when I would turn sixteen and move over to the independent living side of the house. The months leading up to this great anticipated release were tense and difficult, putting us both into a state of perpetual irritation.

For me, the sense of imprisonment in Janet's house and the desire to get out became all the more acute that summer after my sophomore year—because, for the first time, I started seeing a really serious boyfriend.

My High School Boyfriend

HE CALLED ME out of the blue.

He had a kind of high-pitched voice, so at first I thought he was one of the little boys I worked with at the municipal day camp.

"Hi. My name is Dan. Is it okay that I'm calling you? My friends speak highly of you. You seem like an interesting person."

"Hi."

"I saw you written up in the newspaper. For scoring goals in the soccer play-offs. For indoor track. You were second or third in the long jump."

"Second."

"Yeah. And fourth in the state in the three-hundred-meter dash."

"Gee, you really have read up on me."

"I also saw you at a party once . . . and I passed you on Main Street . . . and I remember you came to the basketball games."

"Oh! Right! Basketball! When I was in, like, eighth grade, weren't you the big three-point shooter?"

"Yeah, that's me."

I couldn't place this Dan guy, but I knew I knew him. Since I associated him with basketball, I kept thinking he must be gigantically tall. We talked for a long time. Usually when you talk to someone you don't know, it's pause, pause, awkward pause. You feel so uncomfortable. But he constantly had something to talk about. He was entering his junior year at college, and everything he said was happy and positive. I really liked that.

"Would you go out with me one night this summer? We'd maybe go with another couple someplace."

"I don't know about that. I mean, I don't know you, I can't place you, we've never met, I've never gone out with anybody I've never met before."

"I could come by your house."

"No. Janet's house is not a place you can just come by. Let me think about it. Give me your number. I'll call you in a week."

The whole thing made me nervous. Janet's inviolable curfews and the prying eyes of so many other kids made dating a big hassle at the house on Silver Street. In fact, I had barely dated for that reason. Somehow I had become extremely picky—maybe because I just didn't want to deal with someone who would bring me down when I was trying so hard to stay up. If you weren't really crazy about a guy, it wasn't worth the trouble. I had always liked dating guys who were older—probably a hangup left over from my fatherless babyhood—so I really did want to go out with this junior in college who sounded so nice on the phone. But on the other hand, I was scared.

I just stirred it around all week. And then I called him back and said, "Okay."

I had no idea what to expect. My Silver Street brothers and sisters were as curious as I was, because I never brought guys home, and they were always bugging me about dating. They lurked inside, peeking out from between the slats in the blinds to see what he would be like.

Suddenly one of the guys exclaimed, "Jesus Louisus, Charlotte! Is that your date?!"

There he was, driving up in a white Mustang with tinted windows. I couldn't believe it. This guy got out of this beautiful car and he was not a dork—and he wasn't gigantically tall, either. He was a cute guy with light brown curly hair and eyes so blue you could see them shining in the driveway. The minute I saw him, I realized why he had been such a famous basketball player in our high school. Mighty Dan, the regular-sized guy with the king-size shots.

We got in his car and rode around for the longest time, just talking. We drove over to his house, a big beautiful brick house right near the town center. You wouldn't dream that there was a back yard there, but there is, with a lawn and trees and flowers and a pool and a hammock and a basketball court and a boxer named Louie in his own doghouse.

It was evening, sunset time. The sky was pink. A gorgeous time. When I saw the swimming pool with flowers around it, how clean and well-cared-for everything was, I felt as if I had landed in an oasis in a desert.

Dan's best friend was there with his date, and I knew her, so that made it easy to talk. We drove to a beautiful lake and just sat around and gabbed for a while, watching the moon rise. After a while the other couple left. Dan wanted to show me his favorite spots. We did a lot of driving through the starlit countryside. We went back to his house and watched TV. It was such a laid-back easy date! I was so happy. I felt as if I had known Dan forever.

"Oh my God! It's eleven-thirty! I've got to be home!"

"Okay, fine, no sweat."

"No, no, you don't understand! I've got, like, 120 seconds to be in Janet's house! If I'm late, I lose time out!"

He drove me home. I said I had a good time. He said he'd like to see me again. I said OK and gave him a kiss. Lucky for me it was dark, because my face must have been scarlet.

After that, Dan and I started going out regularly. I spent a lot of time at his house. He had several brothers and sisters. Some of them were married, and they brought their families to visit, so there were lots of nieces and nephews, too. His mother was an energetic Latina woman who served huge meals and also ran her own business. His father was an outgoing man of Lebanese descent whose many friends were always dropping in to discuss their problems and seek advice.

Dan was my first real love. He was my inspiration. I had never known anybody with so much enthusiasm, who was not afraid to just do things and enjoy life. He was so into making the most of himself. And he was very close to his family. I had dreamed of a boyfriend just like him, with a big-hearted family just like his—people from hot climates, sunshiny people who would welcome me and make me feel at home. You know how in the Song of Songs, King Solomon talks about "my sister, my love . . ." I don't think he meant a literal sister. I think he meant a girl who had so much in common with him and his family that she could be like a daughter in the house of his parents.

That was how I felt with Dan's family.

When Dan held me, I felt safe.

When he told me I was beautiful, I didn't just feel like he was some creep paying me compliments so he could get something out of me. I felt *really* beautiful.

I felt more beautiful that summer than ever before.

And maybe that was one reason I had the courage to answer the ad for the pageant.

Five Hundred and Ninety-five Dollars

SO THERE I was, in the late summer between my sophomore and junior years of high school, just hanging out on a sunny Sunday morning, reading the newspaper, dreaming about escaping from my little life, when I saw this ad for the Miss Vermont Teen USA Pageant. *Come and try out!* it said. *You can be on national television with Dick Clark!* And there was an 800 number you could call.

I felt this tremendous rush of excitement. When I got to choose a show to watch at Janet's house, it was invariably *Star Search* or the Miss Universe Pageant or the Miss Teen USA Pageant. No one else knew anything about beauty contests, but I got a lot of the kids interested. Because of me, Janet became interested too.

"Janet, look, there's an advertisement for that pageant we watch!"

"Oh yeah? Really."

"Should I call them?"

"Why not?"

"I'm scared."

"Why? What have you got to lose?"

"I don't know . . . it's not that easy . . ."

"Of course it is. You go out and try it. You'll win, or you won't win, and that's that. Come on, Charlotte. Don't wimp out. Go for it."

"Okay," I said. "Okay. I'll call them."

And then it took me another hour or so before I had the courage to pick up the phone.

When I finally did, I got lucky. A really nice woman answered: Andrea Williams. She worked at the Barbizon School of Modeling, which was running the Miss Teen USA state pageants in Vermont, Massachusetts, New Hampshire, and Maine. Usually you have to send pictures and a little statement about yourself. But something about my phone call made her say, "Tell me about yourself, Charlotte."

And I love to talk. So I did. I told her the whole story of my life, starting from the beginning. Andrea asked me what I looked like and I said I was five feet five inches, that I weighed 117 pounds, with long brown hair and blue eyes, that I would send her a picture right away. She told me that in order to go to Burlington and participate in the event, I had to raise an entry fee of $595.

"Whoa! Two weeks! $595! Janet! Help! What am I gonna do?"

"You're gonna raise the money."

"How?"

"By *asking* people for it, dumbo."

I CALLED A girl that I knew from church named Lucy. She was one of the people who had gotten me interested in beauty pageants to begin with because she had been entering them since she was a little girl, and she had actually won once or twice. Because of her, I got on some mailing lists and received lots of advertisements for pageants here and there; there are gazillions you can enter if you have the money, time, courage, and a support system. I had no idea how complex the whole system was. There were so many pageants. I was glad that this was the one that I had finally decided to go for.

She sent me to a lawyer who had once sponsored her for a contest. I told him a little about myself. He gave me $25. I was wild with joy. Of course I went to the Pizza House—everyone goes there to get sponsored. With Lucy on one side and my smart friend Harriet on the other, I headed down Main Street and went door to door. Panache, Star Electric, Harsch Real Estate, Contemporary Classics.

"Hi. I'm Charlotte Lopez. I live at Janet Henry's house. I'm an official entrant representing Bennington in the Miss Vermont Teen contest, and I have to raise $595 as my entry fee. Could you contribute anything? Anything at all?"

Some people just looked at me as though I were crazy.

Some people just said "No."

Some people said "Sure" and opened the cash register and put $5 in my hand. Or maybe $10. When that happened, I was so astonished that I could barely stammer out my thanks.

I hated every minute of it.

Raising that money was like a total negation of everything I had ever wanted for my life. I wanted independence. I wanted not to need anybody. And here I was, asking complete strangers for money, for this pageant I wasn't even sure I was going out for. If it hadn't been for Lucy and Harriet, trotting me down the street like Clint Eastwood and the Secret Service, I would never have been able to do it.

At the end of a week, I still had a couple of hundred dollars to go.

"I cannot continue with this, Janet. It is so humiliating!"

"You have to go for this, Charlotte! You can't depend on Lucy or Harriet. You have to make it happen for yourself. You can't just crump out; you've got to ask and ask and go and win!"

Harriet's parents and their friends gave me money. My bosses at the ice cream stand helped out, and so did Janet. Bill Wensley called me when he found out I was doing the pageant. He asked me to go out for ice cream with him. I agreed and we went to Friendly's, and he gave me $50. I thought that was very nice of him. We talked a bit, and he wished me the best of luck and said that he knew I was going to do great. It felt good to know that he was supporting me. I raised $50 here, $25 there. Grammy Peterson, who was friendly with Janet, not only gave me money herself but raised it from others as well. She introduced me to a fraternal organization—the Eagles—who gave me $100 and sent me a good-luck note. Little by little I put together the $595.

But then there was this big problem of not having anything to wear. I was known as a nice dresser in my school, but I wore only casual clothes. For the pageant, you needed dressy clothes, business wear. They gave us a whole list of things that we should bring. I bought a plain black bathing suit for a few dollars from Second Hand Rose in downtown Bennington. I borrowed the rest from a school friend named Peaches, who just so happened to have a generous soul and a size four wardrobe. But then I needed an evening gown. Lucky for me that Grammy had a friend at Bridal Fantasy. She was willing to give me a beautiful dress—but it was a size 12! To my delight, this gifted woman altered the dress so that it fit me perfectly. I tried to make my hair more glamorous by putting blonde streaks in it. But the roots were getting dark. So the lady in the beauty shop helped me out by lightening the roots—only she lightened them too much, so they turned sort of white. So now I felt that I looked like a skunk.

But what the hell, I said to myself; I didn't have any particular hopes of winning anyway. I had been trained by long experience never to get my hopes up. When I thought about possibly being Miss Vermont Teen USA, I didn't get excited. I was afraid that in a flash, the whole thing would be over, I'd lose and go home, and I would have wasted all that energy on hoping. So I hoped for nothing except a couple of laughs and a fun night in a new town.

Everybody assumed that Janet would go with me to Burlington. But then all of a sudden, she fell ill with a serious condition called diverticulitis. Tearful and disappointed, she called Grammy Peterson and asked her to accompany me. So off we went to Burlington, me and Harriet and Grammy in Grammy's car.

The Burlington Pageant

THERE WERE TWENTY-ONE contestants for Miss Vermont Teen USA, and another eleven older girls competing to represent Vermont in the Miss USA Pageant.

My roommate had long golden hair and pale porcelain skin with pale freckles. She said she came from a large family with a couple of kids from each of her parents' several marriages and that she lived in a mansion with servants. I felt if I touched her, she would shatter.

"Oh, I am so nervous about this pageant, Charlotte," she said breathlessly.

"Relax. Have fun."

"You're so cool."

"I'm not really; it just looks that way."

I felt completely disorganized compared with my roomate. She had a big Caboodles makeup box, because she had won a year's supply in some other pageant. I had just thrown what little makeup I owned into a little plastic bag. And her dress! It was all tulle and lace and ruffles. Mine was strapless with a slit up the side. She looked like Scarlett O'Hara. I felt like Mae West.

What made me most uncomfortable was the feeling that I came from a different social class than all the other girls. Maybe they didn't know about the thrift-shop bathing suit and the borrowed dresses. But I did. At Janet's house, I always felt very feminine, because all the other girls there were really rough. But the girls at the pageant were way beyond me in terms of feminine. They had great fingernails; I had gnawed mine down to nothing. They had fantastic underwear—I had never set foot inside a Victoria's Secret. As usual, I was riddled with envy for every little thing everybody else had that I felt I lacked.

131

But meeting them all—seeing the range of people, hearing about their lives, singing with them, gabbing with them, comparing stories of boyfriends and teachers—was as invigorating for me as if I had visited Paris or Nairobi. I met a girl who wanted to sneak out of the hotel and meet some guys at a bar. I met a girl who was a secret smoker. I met a girl who was a preacher's kid, who had her heart fixed on the stage. She was a rebel in her family just as I had been in mine. I saw a girl who was absolutely a total knockout destroy her chances of winning when she opened her mouth and turned out to have nothing to say. Just by being with those girls, I learned how personality and intellect had the power to make a plain girl irresistible.

Some of us rehearsed while others of us had interviews. The judges were in the hotel ballroom. They sat in a big U, and we went from one to the next. We had four minutes with each judge. I went from judge to judge—twelve judges, all different. They asked me questions about who I was, what I liked to do, what I thought. I tried to give coherent answers that weren't too hokey.

We rehearsed the whole stage setup. The Barbizon people gave the directions: where to stand, where to walk, how to turn, how to look at the judges. The cardinal rule was this: *When you walk out on stage, you have to look at the judges the whole time.*

I promised myself I would do that—I kept repeating the rule over and over to myself—but when we got into the final stages of the pageant on Sunday night and looked out at the audience in the hall, all I could think was, *Where are Grammy and Harriet?*

When I made it into the final twelve, I knew Grammy would be patting her bosom, trying to calm her racing heart, and Harriet would be squirming in her seat. When I made it into the final six, I knew Grammy would be cautioning her, "Now don't go getting too excited, Harriet dear, because our Charlotte is still very far from winning."

I came down the runway and turned. I knew that I was supposed to look at the judges. But I had to see Grammy and Harriet! Where were they? At the end of the runway, I turned left instead of right as I was supposed to. And there they were, right in front of me. I couldn't stop grinning at them, which was exactly what I was not supposed to do.

I guess the judges didn't hold that against me, because a few minutes later, I was Miss Vermont Teen USA.

Winning . . . and Losing

WHEN I CAME back to school on Monday, I was a celebrity. All the Vermont papers carried a picture of me with a crown and a sash and a huge bunch of flowers. I went up and down the streets of our little town, thanking everybody who had helped me. What fun that was! To see all the people so happy! To be a little famous!

At school, everybody said, You're so special, so pretty. They had this attitude: Wow, she's a beauty queen! Everyone heard about the prizes I had won. Three thousand dollars to buy my wardrobe for the national finals the following summer in Mississippi, and an all-expenses-paid round trip to Biloxi. A trophy and a plaque. All the Hawaiian Tropic tanning products any girl could possibly want. A one-year scholarship to the Barbizon Modeling School.

(Funny about that—the Wensleys had promised to send me there one day, but it had never happened. And now I had the chance to go to Barbizon because of my own efforts, my own victory. I never went, because as time passed, going to college became much more important to me than going to modeling school. But the Barbizon scholarship was like a sign to me that no one can make your life happen for you. You have to do it yourself.)

The kids at school admired me and envied me and thought I was a major big deal. Strange as it may seem, it's not an entirely pleasant feeling.

I mean, I liked it . . . but I didn't like it.

Lots of guys wanted to go out with me, but most of them were too intimidated to ask. I hated feeling that I couldn't just sit with my girlfriends and talk to them. Some of them were cool with the Miss Vermont Teen USA thing. But some were afraid and jealous and a little dangerous. How could I explain to all these people who were so envious that I had spent the last moments of the pageant in Burlington looking desperately all over the hall for Grammy and Harriet, who at that moment in that place represented all I had to call "my family"?

It was ten months until the National Miss Teen USA Pageant in Biloxi. I didn't do a lot of Vermont functions, because there weren't a lot to do. I didn't have to raise money for the next round. I was given everything I needed to go to the nationals. I worked out as I always did. I went to school. I tried to deal with the hatred of the girls who would never forgive me for turning out to be a beauty queen, one of whom was turning out to be my old friend Marcy.

The Downside of a Great Year

MY JUNIOR YEAR in high school was terrific. I had a lot of really great friends, I did well in sports and academics, I had what I considered enough pocket money. My adorable boyfriend Dan was mature and caring. He gave me confidence and a sense of security. So did my extraordinary experience at the pageant in Burlington. Now, instead of being thought of as a loser whose family had tossed her into a home for juvenile delinquents, I was the big winner on every scorecard. I was in the Homecoming Court. I was Prom Queen. I looked forward to a huge fun time at the National Miss Teen USA Pageant in Biloxi the following summer—and in my wildest, most secret dreams, I imagined winning the pageant and the treasure of scholarships that would enable me to go to college.

But for a good year, it sure had some wicked downsides.

My ex–best friend Marcy, along with her sidekicks Cocoa and Pat, went to every length to harass me and make my life miserable. Things had started going bad between us back in the days right after I moved out of the Wensleys, when Cocoa and Marcy got me fired. Things got worse during my sophomore year, when I became friends with Harriet and the "preppy crowd." When I took Harriet with me to the Burlington pageant, Marcy probably felt totally miffed. With Cocoa telling her "Charlotte's so full of herself. She thinks she's such hot shit now . . ." and Pat saying "I told you so," our estrangement turned to real enmity.

Life in school became a nightmare because of that. Everywhere I went, there they were—Marcy the Angry, Pat the Jealous, Cocoa the Tagalong—like three witches dropping curses in my path. When I passed them in the hall, they would whisper, "Slut! Bitch!" I would pretend I didn't notice and walk on past. That made them even even more furious. So when I was down the hall, they would yell, "Slut! Bitch!" and every insecure girl in the school would turn around and think, *Is somebody yelling that at* me?

At lunch, Pat stared at me. I would be eating with friends and she would just stare at me. I ignored her. Still, every time I went to lunch, I got butterflies in my stomach. I hated having to deal with so much immaturity. The only thing I had done "wrong" was to make something of my life—unlike these fools, whose only entertainment was to get high and harass those they envied.

I wasn't the only one they went after. They picked on kids from good families who had good manners and who they thought wouldn't fight back. Kids like Harriet, and Peaches, who had lent me clothes, and Lucy, who had given me so much advice before the pageant.

The Witches also hated my new locker mate, Vera, a jolly girl who was such a good athlete that some colleges were already recruiting her. They would leave foul, threatening messages on Vera's answering machine, just to frighten and offend her mother and her kid sisters.

One day I opened my locker and smelled this horrendous stench! Someone had put Buck Lure in there! It's this stuff that hunters use to attract the big deer in the forest.

"Vera! Stay back! Don't touch the locker!"

"Yuch! Charlotte! You smell like deer piss!"

"How am I gonna get it off?"

"Those bitches! That's it. I've had enough."

"Vera! What are you gonna do? Vera! Come on, we've got to ignore this, we've got to be mature!"

She took off down the hall, mad as hell. Before I knew it, some of our guy friends had been alerted to the incident. And soon, whether we liked it or not (okay, okay, we loved it!), we were being avenged by this trio of heroes—Sam, Hank, and Marshall. These guys were like the modern version of the Green Mountain Boys. They loved ski racing, hunting, football, trucks, and motorcycles—and they got pretty good grades too. I liked to call them the Shit Kickers, in honor of the big heavy boots that they wore with their jeans and their baseball caps. When they walked down the halls together, the lockers would tremble and quake.

"What are you guys up to?"

"Don't worry, Charlotte."

"Come on, fellas . . ."

"We'll take care of everything."

I went to a dentist appointment. When I came back to school, Cocoa was screaming in the locker hall. Her face was purple.

"Charlotte, you bitch! You're dead! You and Vera put Buck Lure *and* sardines on our locker!"

I tried to keep a straight face.

"I don't know what you're talking about; I was not even here."

I walked away with my shoulders back and my head held high, trying to look cool and elegant. But inside I was squealing, *Way to go, Shit Kickers!*

AIR BAND NIGHT is a really big event at our school, and the gym was packed. Harriet, Vera, Peaches, Lucy, and I worked up two dances to "Rump Shaker," this really dirty rap song. We practiced at Harriet's grandfather's house. We got costumes together—shorts and sparkly tank tops—and when we did the act, the whole school cracked up. The Witches stewed in their jealousy.

We made it to the finals of the air band competition. As we went upstairs into the sound booth to get our "Rump Shaker" tape, we passed Marcy and Cocoa, who were coming down. They didn't say anything to us. But Harriet looked in the tape deck and saw that our tape was missing. Cool, calm, together Harriet just freaked out. She ran downstairs and caught up with Marcy and Cocoa in the cafeteria.

"Marcy! Did you take our air band tape?"

"No."

"Cocoa?"

"Of course not, jerk."

"Oh yeah? So what's this?"

And she pulled the tape right out of Cocoa's shirt pocket.

I just wanted to run away from there and forget it. However, Harriet told a cop what had happened, and the cop made the Three Witches go home.

We went on and did our show and somebody else won, but it didn't matter, because it was just so much fun. Except I kept seeing Marcy's face, how mad she was, how betrayed she felt, and I just didn't know how to stop this thing.

It got to the point where I went to the principal about it. I begged him to intervene; I mean, I felt that I shouldn't have to go to school and listen to these girls harassing me for no reason, and I was furious that my friends got the same treatment by association. If a boy had been harassing me, they might have been able to do something about it. But the way it was . . . what could the principal do, anyway?

Every week there was something.

Janet's son and I went Rollerblading, and Marcy came by in her car and tried to run us off the road.

Vera and her boyfriend went to a party, and Marcy came charging up to them accusing them of banging into her car—which they hadn't done—and when they left the party, Marcy and Cocoa ran up to Vera and threatened to poke her eyes out with a windshield wiper.

Pat was the prettiest of the Three Witches—and still the most insecure—and she couldn't seem to let go of the idea that I was competing with her for guys. Her new boyfriend was famous in school for being a womanizer. She thought he had a crush on me. Maybe he did, but I sure wasn't the only one! Pat kept insinuating that I was trying to take him away from her. I had to endure this stupid, childish campaign of whispers, threatening notes, and anonymous phone messages.

One day, a whole bunch of senior girls just got so fed up with

Pat and her slimy whispers that they ganged up and told her off, right out in the courtyard in front of everybody. I guess it was the end for Pat the Jealous.

I hated the whole conflict with the Three Witches.

People told me that it was just because they were jealous—that Pat hated me because she was jealous, and Cocoa was a follower, and Marcy hated me because I was hanging around with new people and she was being manipulated by these other two girls. Jealousy, everybody said. Jealousy.

Even if that was true, it didn't make it hurt any less.

I still miss Marcy—that's the truth. In the days when we were friends, I cherished her and needed her and maybe I clung too close and turned her away from me. I don't hate her for any of the bad things that passed between us; I cared about her too much when we were friends to hate her now or ever.

So This Is Independent Living!

AT THE BEGINNING of my junior year, when I was sixteen, I had moved to the independent living side of Janet's house, with great expectations that my life would change. It hadn't. At least not enough to seem meaningful to me.

Janet didn't base her rules on trust and on how long you were there. She based them on age. If you were sixteen, you could go out once during the week and once on weekends. If you were seventeen, you could go out every other day. You needed two days' notice before you could go anywhere. You could be out for only three hours at a time during the week, four hours during the weekend. No more than two phone calls a day for ten minutes each. I had lived with Janet for more than two years, and I still had very few more privileges than a sixteen-year-old who had come in off the street last month.

The only way to improve the situation was to do extra chores and get a "happy face" put up by your name on the roster in the kitchen. And what was a happy face worth anyway? A big extra half hour on the outside!

That's often the trouble with foster care. You try to be like a normal kid. Try to improve your situation. But in a fixed and rigid system, there's no room for improvement, and there's no reward for it either.

"I hate the rules."

"Well, too bad, Charlotte. Everybody has to live by them."

"I've proved myself. I shouldn't have to live by them in the same way as the other kids."

"If I make an exception for you, I'll have a revolt on my hands."

We had these arguments all the time—every other day, it seemed. I always wanted to go out more, be with my friends more, see Dan for a longer stretch of time, be more spontaneous. So many times I wanted to do something but couldn't because I didn't have two days' notice. Sometimes if I was lucky and Janet was in a good mood, she would let that slip and make an exception. But not often enough for me. I wrote Janet a ten-page letter about it. I wasn't saying the rules were bad. I was just saying that for me they were bad. I felt like I was on parole, and I told her that. I didn't yell. I was very mature. But she was set in her ways.

Janet's rules were made for lost boys and wayward girls. For them, structure was order, and order was sanity. But I didn't have their problems. Besides, I felt that I was special. When I came home from the Burlington pageant, Janet was feeling so ill that all the kids in the house had to be placed elsewhere. Her son Jon and I and two wonderful girls, who roomed near me on the independent living side, stayed and took care of her. One of the girls cooked, one kept house, I watched Janet's grandson Krissie, and Jon took care of everything else. The other kids came back after Janet got well, but we three independent living girls who stayed always felt more part of Janet's family than they did.

There were times during my junior year when I was so fed up with Janet's rules, I would say I was going to the store and climb to the top of the hill and use the pay phone and call Dan at college. If I didn't have enough change, I'd use the calling card number that Marcy had once given me and some of her other friends, figuring I'd pay her back when the bill came.

I'd sit on the phone with Dan and weep from sheer frustration and helplessness.

I couldn't stand the way we were living.

And there was nothing we could do!

In December, right before Christmas, I did something I would never have done before with any of my previous social workers. I wrote Angela a letter. I wanted her to know that I had a problem, that I needed another way of life, a different home.

Angela probably knew I didn't belong at Janet's. She just didn't have the time to make the effort to get me out. So I had to flag her down somehow, explode myself into a priority spot on her crowded caseload.

December 13, 1992

Dear Angela,

This is Charlotte writing to you. I've had some things on my mind, and I thought writing to you would be better than trying to get hold of you.

Two years ago, when I walked into Janet's house, I had no idea what to expect. I had no idea it was a group home or even what a group home was. All I knew was that I was going to a home where religion wasn't going to be shoved down my throat, and I was going to be able to lead a normal teenager's life.

Well, the couple of weeks that I was supposed to be at Janet's turned into months. I found it hard to adjust to the rules of a group home. But I did the best I could. I think the biggest reason I did so well was because Janet told me when I was sixteen, I could move over onto the independent living side. She made it sound so wonderful. She said it was a great privilege to be over there . . . where we would have more privileges, be more independent, and have more freedom.

This opportunity sounded great. It gave me something to work for. So for the following year and a half, I worked hard to earn Janet's trust and to show her that I was a mature and responsible young woman. As you know, I achieved this goal. I have had a lot of good things happen to me because of my maturity and responsibility, and I have had only a few minor problems in the two years I've been here.

But Angela, I haven't seen any of the great benefits that Janet has been raving about happening. The only thing that's different about independent living is that you're in a different part of the house. I know Janet's been sick lately, but how hard is it to award kids like me . . . the freedom and independence that we worked so hard for?!

I feel cheated. I don't belong in a group home. Maybe all these rules are required for strange teenagers coming into Janet's house with major problems. But for me, I feel they're unreasonable. And also for the other girls who live in independent living as well. We have talked it over a great deal and are all feeling the same way.

I guess the reason why it's been on my mind the most lately is because Christmas vacation is coming up. I don't want to be sitting around the house doing nothing when I could be spending quality time with Dan and other friends who are coming home from college for winter break.

Even my sister is allowed to go as she wants if she can find something that'll keep her busy instead of sitting on her butt at home. I think a lot of that had to do with me leaving, but nevertheless, she's allowed to do that as long as she's in at curfew. . . . I've been living with Janet and her rules for so long that it seems like I'm asking for a lot. But I'm really not, Angela. I'm really just asking to be able to do the things that all my friends are doing.

It would be the best Christmas present ever.

Charlotte Lopez

The Best Christmas Present Ever

WELL, I WAS wrong.

The best Christmas present ever turned out to be the reunion Diana and I had with our brother, Duane. Over the years I was growing up, I'd think of Duane every once in a while. It wasn't as if I really missed him. I just thought that being apart from him was the way it was supposed to be. But as a sixteen-year-old, feeling estranged from my previous family and alienated from the group family that was being offered to me, I once again started thinking about my brother.

It all began the summer before. SRS had never done anything to keep us in touch with Duane. So I asked my boss at the ice cream stand to call Duane's foster mother, Carol Wehner, on my behalf. It turned out that for all the years we were at the Wensleys', he lived only twenty minutes away! From that phone call I received Duane's new address in Colorado, and I wrote to him. He didn't answer right away. Carol says he had some doubts about a reunion, that it brought up a lot of memories he would rather have buried. But then he sent me a T-shirt and a tape that his band had made. And Carol ran into my sister Diana at a soccer game, and they got to talking, and soon the reunion was arranged. We would meet at Carol's house when Duane came home to Vermont around Christmastime.

I had it all planned. I would spend the afternoon with Dan at the mall, and in the evening I would go meet Duane. I had enough "happy faces" for five hours out that afternoon, and since time-outs with family never counted, I figured I could stay at Carol Wehner's house until the regular evening curfew.

As I was going outside, Janet said, "You can't do that."

"What do you mean?"

"You can't go to the mall for five hours and then spend the evening out as well. You have to choose. You can either go with Dan for five hours or with Duane."

"I haven't been out all week long."

"You know the rules. You can split the time between them if you want, but you only have five hours total."

I couldn't believe she was serious. But she was.

Maybe she was just having a bad day. Or maybe it was one of those jealousy things foster parents get into—because we were going to Carol Wehner's house, and Bill Wensley was taking us, so where was Janet in this picture? Nowhere. I know that when people who aren't really mean act mean, it's usually because they're feeling hurt. Maybe I had hurt Janet when I wrote to Angela. But at that moment I didn't care. This was the biggest day of my life! And Janet seemed to have no concept of how important it was to me!

I stood in the kitchen and started to scream and cry as I hadn't done since I was a little girl.

"Now, Charlotte, cut it out, stop bawling."

"Ahhhh! Ahhhhhhhhhhh!"

"Oh, for heaven's sakes!"

Janet stomped out of the kitchen and went into her room and closed the door. I called Dan and wailed on the phone to him. He tried to console me, said we'd see each other another time, that the important thing was for me to meet Duane. I knew he was right, but the unfairness of it all just made me crazy. I fled to the independent living side of the house and pressed "record" on a tape recorder and poured my heart onto the tape, just the way I had poured my heart out to my stuffed animals at the Wensleys'. All I wanted to do was run away! But I couldn't, because I was a ward of the state and if I ran, the cops would come after me and I would end up in the lockup with the fire starters and the child molesters, and the Wensleys would get to say "We told you so!" to everybody in Bennington, and I wouldn't get to go to Biloxi to the Miss Teen USA National Pageant, and I wouldn't get to see Dan or my sister or my brother Duane or go to college, and everything I had worked for would be gone!

Janet appeared in my doorway. Her eyes were glistening with tears. But I didn't care. I was over the edge. Hysterical.

"I don't know why you are getting all worked up over this. You know the rules and I can't change them."

"The hell with the rules! They are for sick crazy people and juvenile delinquents! I am Charlotte! I am a normal kid! You said you loved me but you are treating me like a criminal! HOW CAN YOU TREAT ME THIS WAY?!"

DIANA AND BILL Wensley picked me up at six. I was in a miserable mood to begin with, and the fact that this reunion wasn't going to include just me and my sister made it worse. So when I finally looked my brother in the face after a dozen years of separation, I probably wasn't as excited as I might have been. His foster home, where he had lived for all those years, was in Manchester, only a short drive away. I couldn't believe he'd been so close for so long.

Duane came downstairs. We just looked at him. He just looked at us. He had these strange boots on—a cross between sneakers and hiking boots. And a purple-gray sweatshirt. He had blue eyes. We looked a lot alike. It was so much more laid back than I thought it was going to be. It was like, "Hi, how are you doing?" Duane brought us into the kitchen. And Bill stayed. I was so angry he stayed with us. At *my* family reunion! And he had a beer! Drinking was one of the worst things you could do in the Wensley house. And now, for Bill to just sit down and have a beer with Duane and his foster mother like a regular person—it blew me away!

Duane made linguini with a terrific sauce. Diana played the piano. She talked about soccer and school. Carol Wehner recalls that Bill was "personable and wonderful and delightful," that she had no idea I was uncomfortable about him being there. But I was angry because I felt that I had arranged this meeting —finding Duane's address, writing to him—and now Bill was making it sound like the whole thing happened because Carol met Diana at a soccer game and arranged it all with him and Cari! I felt I got no credit for any of it, that I was just along for the ride.

After some time Bill left, and then I talked about what was really on my mind. I wanted to be adopted. Carol told me to consider the Wensleys, because she felt that they really cared a lot about me. But she had no idea about my situation with them. I was long past that point. I wanted to have a new family—a family that was good for the person I had turned out to be.

Duane took us home in his truck. Diana sat in the front and I sat in the back and we just talked and talked and talked the whole way. About school. About the pageant. Even though it had been in the papers and in our conversation, I really don't think Duane realized I had won Miss Vermont Teen USA until we were sitting in that truck together.

"Wait a minute, wait a minute. You won that thing!"

"Yeah."

"So now you're going to the finals in Biloxi and you're going to be on TV!"

"Yeah."

"You won the freaking beauty contest!"

"Right, Duane. Watch the road."

It was a few minutes past ten when we got to Janet's house.

She came out of her room, eager to hear how the evening had gone. But I just said good night and closed my door. I knew I was hurting her—but I couldn't stop myself. It was *my* life, *my* family, *my* evening. I didn't want to share it.

I sat on my bed in the independent living side of the house and wondered what was going to become of me. It was so dark. Such a cold, dark, bleak Vermont winter night. I thought maybe this was all my fault; maybe I would never be happy living anywhere. All these homes I had been in—the pattern was always the same. Living with the Wensleys was fine growing up, but then afterward . . . Then at Janet's house, good things happened, but a lot of the stuff was not very fun. Something always turned me off to a home. And now I was right back where I always seemed to end up—alone with my own insecurities in a boiling pot of envy.

I envied Duane because of the life he had had with Carol Wehner. Her house was filled with pictures of the trips her family had taken. You could see how close he was to her kids, the love, the bonding.

I envied Diana because things were so much easier for her now that I had left the Wensleys; they were more lenient, more forgiving with her than they had ever been with me; and soon she would be their adopted daughter.

As far as I could see, everybody had a family except me.

Maybe I was too picky.

Maybe I was too much of a pain in the butt.

Maybe it was all my fault.

I figured I had two options in this world. I could "age out" of the system and live alone on my own. Miss Teen Nowhere. Or I could somehow convince Angela and her colleagues at Social and Rehabilitation Services of Vermont to make one last effort to find me a family.

CHAPTER *Six*

ANGELA STOPPED BY at Janet's house a few days after Christmas and found me really upset and angry. I told her I simply had to have a family. I wanted a mom and dad and either just myself or one other kid. I was bound and determined that one way or another, I was going to college, and when I came home for vacation, I wanted a family to come home to, a family home where I could bring my friends, parents who would always be there and who would be grandparents for my own children.

She promised me that in six or eight weeks, she would get together with Valerie Miner, the resource coordinator of SRS in Bennington, and they would would start looking for an adoptive home for me. Six weeks went by and nothing happened. I asked again, and more weeks went by. I felt edgy, impatient, fearful that the system would once more forget me. The "rest of my life" obsessed me. Everybody else was set, and I was nowhere. How could I arrange to have a family to share the future with?

Then, toward the end of that winter, something happened that almost guaranteed that I would have no future at all.

One Last Attempt by Charlotte to Screw Up Everything

I WAS STANDING in the kitchen, wearing cut-offs and a T-shirt and doing the dishes, when a cop car pulled up to the house. No big deal. Cops came over all the time. We gave them cookies. But this cop was different. I could hear him in the front room, saying to Janet, "I'm here for Charlotte Lopez."

I froze. My heart stopped. I had no clue to what was going on. All I could think was, *My God, you did something, you did something illegal! WHAT THE HELL DID YOU DO?!*

"Charlotte! This policeman is here because they're claiming you stole Marcy's mother's calling card. Is that true?"

I breathed a sigh of relief.

"Oh, that—that's nothing. Of course I didn't steal Marcy's mother's calling card. Marcy gave me and some other kids the number when we were friends. I think at the time she was doing it to get back at her mom for something. She said I could use it whenever I wanted."

As I was blithely explaining this whole story, Janet and the policeman looked increasingly upset.

"Are you crazy, Charlotte? Do you realize that it is a crime to use somebody else's calling card?"

"A crime? No way! I didn't even know how to use the calling card when Marcy and I were friends. But when our friendship ended, when I started seeing Dan, and he was at school three hours away, it was really convenient to have a calling card number to call him on, so somebody told me how to use the number and I used it, and I figured that when the bill came, I would pay."

I was babbling and they were staring at me as though I were totally out of my mind.

"This calling card has been reported stolen, Charlotte. STOLEN!"

"Oh, come on. How could I have stolen it? I would have had to break into Marcy's house or somehow find her mother's pocketbook or wallet or wherever she kept the card, and I couldn't have done that because by the time I started using the number, Marcy and I weren't friends anymore, we were total enemies, and I was never invited to her house, and I was never anywhere near her mother."

A look of terror was beginning to appear on Janet's face.

"Marcy's mother claims you put over $800 on her phone bill!"

"Oh, I couldn't possibly have run up that big a bill. I only used it to call Dan; he's not that far away. Don't worry, I'll pay the bill and that'll be that."

I was totally calm. Janet was frantic. She kept trying to explain to me why what I had done was illegal. Somehow, I kept failing to understand.

"Look, I've got the money. I'll go to the bank and get the money right now. . . . What's the big deal?"

As I stood there, with Janet wringing her hands and the big cop with his gun and his cuffs just staring down at me, it finally got through that this was turning out to be a very big deal indeed. Marcy and her family were saying that I had stolen the card. That was like a major crime, a federal offense. I suddenly started to wonder why I hadn't used it when we were friends and had used it so frequently when we were bitter enemies. Maybe I thought that when her mother saw all those calls and realized Marcy had given out the number, she would be furious, and Marcy would be in big trouble.

Fantasies. Teenage fantasies.

When the bill came in, Marcy told her mother I had stolen the card, and now I was the one in big trouble.

The police asked me questions about how I got the number. I told them everything. They told me that if I was charged, I could be thrown out of the pageant. Angela looked at me with a grim expression and said, "You did a delinquent thing, Charlotte. A really serious delinquent thing. You need to write a letter of apology. You need to pay these folks back. Or they are going to press charges against you, and that's not going to look very good with your Miss Vermont Teen title."

It was spring break. When I went back to school, Marcy was always yelling at me in the halls, "I can't believe you used my card! You're a J.D. and thief! You're not worthy to be Miss Teen Anything! You're not going to the national pageant. You're going to court!"

Every day for weeks, Marcy was in my face.

When I walked to school in the mornings, there they were, Cocoa and Marcy in Marcy's white car, cruising alongside me, calling me "Thief!" When I walked through the school courtyard on my way to my afternoon workout, Cocoa would hang with her friends in the phone booth and call out to me in this nasty way: "Wanna make a phone call, Charlotte?"

As the phone company started breaking apart the bill, it turned out that I owed about $150. Clearly other people besides me had used that number too. It was a help to cite the others— but it was no excuse. I had still used something that wasn't mine. I knew I was in the wrong.

Marcy's mother called the pageant people and went on and on about what a terrible person I was. They called me, seriously concerned. Janet and I told them the truth. They could have ditched me right then. But they didn't. They said they would wait and see if any charges were brought against me—and then decide how to deal with the situation.

Then Marcy's mother called up Angela and screamed and yelled that SRS was trying to cover up the scandal. She threatened to go to the papers. Angela replied, "I don't care what the papers say. If it affects Charlotte's title, that will be unfortunate, but I'm not trying to sweep anything under the rug. Charlotte is saying she was given permission to use the number. You're saying she stole it. If you think you can prove that, take it to the district attorney's office."

For about three weeks, Janet and I were really on edge.

And then, suddenly, it was over.

No criminal charges were ever pressed.

I paid back the money from my earnings at the ice cream stand.

It was over.

When I think back now on the whole calling card scandal, I have a little uneasy feeling that deep down in my subconscious, maybe I looked for this trouble.

Is it possible? Is it really possible that I might have tried to offend a girl who I knew already hated me in order to get myself into hot water? So that the cops would come? And my busy, overtaxed social worker would have to put down what she was doing and handle the crisis? Can it be possible that I would endanger my title, my reputation, everything I had worked so hard to achieve so that SRS would have to pay attention to me and get down to it at last and rescue me from family-less-ness?

I can't believe I would do that.

I just can't believe it.

The List Lady

VALERIE MINER, THE SRS resource coordinator, says that foster care at its best helps to draw a "circle of trust" around a child. To put children into the right circles, she keeps a lot of lists. A list of long-term foster parents who were interested in adopting. A list of children whose parental rights were not yet terminated, but who were likely to be adoptable soon. A list of kids like me, who were already free for adoption and needed permanent homes.

She and Angela went through the lists. But they couldn't immediately find any family that would want to adopt a sixteen-year-old who dreamed of being a singer and an actress. So they started writing an ad to put in the newspaper: *Wanted: Family to Adopt Charlotte Lopez.*

Angela remembers thinking it was pretty ridiculous.

Valerie took another look at her lists. And suddenly they noticed someone, a woman named Jill Charles. She had been licensed as a foster parent in 1989 and had already been a foster mother to several different kids. She had gone through the training twice, once as a single parent, once with her new husband, Al Scheps. (The rules had liberalized since Grammy tried to adopt us; now qualified single parents could have foster kids and could also adopt.) Jill knew most of the social workers in Bennington County, and she and Al had become friendly with the other members of the Foster Parents Association. She had helped to organize a fundraiser to purchase duffel bags for the foster children, so that when they journeyed from home to home, they wouldn't have to be dragging their stuff around in plastic bags as I had done.

Jill lived in Dorset, where for almost two decades she had run the well-known Dorset Theatre Festival, a professional summer theater. She was also a writer and publisher, freelancing for theatrical newspapers and regional magazines, and publishing national theater directories for actors and students. Angela and Valerie figured she was "probably the only trained foster parent in Vermont who knew what the William Morris Agency was."

I didn't realize it at the time, but Jill had actually seen me at the annual Christmas party that the Foster Parents Association gives for foster families. My sister Diana and I had entertained there. We sang "Silent Night." I guess we must have made a good impression on her.

"I remember thinking, what a terrific kid this Charlotte Lopez must be," Jill says, "to be living in a group home and still have enough gumption and drive to go out for the pageant and win it. And what a considerate thing for her to do, to come back and entertain for this gang of kids."

Valerie called Jill at the end of April.

The winter thaw had just about passed. Spring was coming.

Honestly, spring in Vermont is like the raising of the dead.

The mountains have been so frozen and so covered with ice and snow, the night has been falling so early, you've been so shut in and entombed in your house with your steaming cups of cocoa and soup that your skin begins to feel sort of thick, and your nose gets permanently numb, like a stick of cold wood— it's been unbelievably long since you've been able to sniff the air without making a cloud or a dribble.

When the thaw comes, you're in mud up to your knees.

But who cares? Winter is ending. The gorgeous winter for which our state is so famous, which brings us our tourists with their skis and snowboards, is finally letting go. And soon the ground firms up, and the sugar sap begins to run from the maple trees. And the daffodils you forgot you planted at the forest edge pop out of the wet brown leaves and twinkle.

It's spring, Charlotte.

Get ready for a new life.

Meeting Jill and Al

I HAD BEEN jogging. I was on the front porch, all sweaty, guzzling Gatorade, on an exercise adrenaline high. Angela came up the path to Janet's house with these two people—Jill and Al. Jill was wearing a white sweater with little flowers on it. She had curly brown hair, just starting to turn a little gray, and a nice smile. She seemed very laid-back and kind. Al was a big growly bear kind of a guy, with lots of wild iron-colored hair and an all-knowing gleam in his eye. He spoke with a pronounced New Jersey accent, and his background was Italian. These people just might be, said Angela, a set of potential adoptive parents.

We visited for a while. I hadn't met many large Italians from New Jersey, so I wasn't so easy with Al, but Jill felt totally familiar to me. Since my idea of family centered on questions of personal liberty, and I always measured parental personalities in terms of who would let you out and who would keep you in, I immediately concocted this whole scenario where Jill was the sweet one who would let me get away with things and Al was this big, gruff, bearlike person who would never let a girl out of the house.

It'll never work, I thought.

I'll always have to go to Jill and beg her to override him. Of course, I didn't say that. I just thought that. I was sixteen years old and I still thought of parents as wardens. A lifetime in the foster care system can do that to a person.

They asked me why I wanted to be adopted.

I told them about a dream that I'd had: I was away at college and it was Christmas and everyone was going home for the holiday and I had nowhere to go.

They asked me if I wanted to spend the weekend with them.

I almost said no.

Can you imagine? I was so afraid of Al Scheps that I almost said no.

But something in Jill's face—some cool, collected thing about her handshake and her smile and her steady gaze—made me say, "Okay." So Angela made the arrangements.

Jill says that when they left me, she and Al talked about adopting. They had some really serious questions. What were they going to wind up with if they adopted me? A starlet? A fashion model? Jill was an intellectual, an artist: was she really the sort of person who could handle that? Al thought maybe I might just want a home until I was eighteen and would then drop out. Jill figured that would be okay if that was what I wanted. After all, she wasn't thinking of adopting a little kid to raise in her image, to shape and mold. She knew she was dealing with a pretty much grown-up person, and the only thing that would keep us together over the long term was not any particular physical or practical dependence, but rather just a good relationship.

And then there were financial considerations. After all, it's no small thing to take on a child only a year away from college. It wasn't as if they had been putting away $25 a week in a tuition fund since I was in diapers.

"But that consideration paled," Jill says, "compared to the emotional need, the family connection Charlotte was after."

For my part, I looked forward to my visit with them. But I didn't want to get up my expectations.

Al and Jill live in beautiful Dorset, a town of only about a thousand people. Incredible mountain vistas, stands of towering pines. They have a cozy white house with little black shutters and massive pine trees all around. You entered up a flight of stairs that took you directly into the kitchen, so by the time you got to the living room, all your cruddy muddy outdoor clothes were off and hanging out to dry someplace. The living room was big, with baby blue carpeting and a gazillion books and cats snoozing on the sofas. In one corner Jill had her office, where she works on the theater directories and many articles that she writes. (She also ghostwrites a monthly column in the *Bennington Banner* that's supposed to be "written" by the Humane Society's main cats, Beaches and Missy.) Al says Jill is one of those people who "got into Phi Beta Kappa and doesn't know where the key is anymore."

Upstairs there were three bedrooms. Out back, there was a big deck facing a broad grassy yard; in the summertime, you could sunbathe out there and enjoy a relaxed alfresco meal. When I first visited Al and Jill, they had a foster child, a boy, who was living with them. He was a little younger than me and very friendly. I slept in a tiny bedroom with a big window.

Around from the back of the house, there are some other houses and the Dorset Colony House, which the theater runs, a haven where lots of writers stay during the winter to work on their books and plays and where some of the stage crew boards during the summer season. And across the street from the house is the small barn that houses the theater itself.

I loved the theater.

The auditorium is built into a hollowed-out barn. On the ceiling over the audience there is a huge old wagon wheel hung with lights, a real Vermont-made chandelier. Jill showed me around backstage. The light booth, the shop where they build the sets, the actors' dressing rooms, the huge costume closets. It had a special smell . . . old makeup, sawdust. Because it was spring, some of the theater people were just arriving to set up things for the new summer season. Jill introduced me to everybody. Very few of those people knew I was Miss Vermont Teen USA or anything. They just thought I was one of Jill's foster kids. They were so warm and friendly to me. I felt instantly at home.

Jill and I sat in the green room where the actors hang out before and after the show, and we just talked. She had a great attitude. She seemed to look on me as though I were a person, not a case; a young woman, not a problem. She wanted to know how I felt about things. Jill also understood from vast personal experience the insecurity of the performer, the love-hate relationship with the limelight, the satisfactions of applause. She didn't hold it against me that I needed attention. She knew lots of people like that.

"I recognized in Charlotte many of my own insecurities," Jill says. "That show business person's need to be loved. The sense of seeming eccentric in the 'normal' world. And also a privacy thing about her, a 'don't-get-too-close-right-now' thing that I have too. But in another regard, we were very different. Because I've never been without the security of a family. I've always known that I could pick up a phone and somebody would be there for me. Charlotte didn't have that security. She needed that kind of home."

When I think about it now, I see that our early meetings were really pretty bizarre. Jill says they felt like auditions. Do you like me enough to be your mother? Do I like you enough to want you for my kid? "Al's reaction was wait and see," Jill says. "But as far as I was concerned, Charlotte and I found the magic almost immediately. Whatever arrangement Charlotte wanted, I was ready for it. Valerie called and we talked about twenty minutes and I said, 'Yes. If she wants to be, Charlotte can be our daughter.' "

When I went back to Janet's after the weekend with Al and Jill, I wasn't excited. I felt sort of calm inside. No butterflies. No *agita*, as Al would say. Just a quiet feeling, like after you eat a good meal and you're full and you're okay.

"How did it go, Charlotte?"

"Oh, it was nice, Janet. It was a really wonderful weekend."

"So you like them, Jill and Al?"

"Yes. Very much."

"Well, that's great, Charlotte. That's great news."

She grinned at me and turned away quickly.

She knew I was bound to leave her. She knew I couldn't stay forever in her kind of family. She had already met Jill Charles and thought she was a wonderful person, figured it would probably be a good match. But her eyes were full of tears.

THROUGHOUT THE SPRING before the national pageant, I would stay weekends with Jill and Al in Dorset. Initially, the town itself scared me. In Vermont, Dorset has the reputation of being full of huge historic houses and the rich people who own them and who spend their time filling them with priceless antiques. In my fantasies of how such people live—which may not be too far from the truth—they come in the summertime and stay for the changing of the leaves in the fall, then in the winter they go someplace warmer just for fun or perhaps to Boston or New York or Europe where they have other houses, and they take care of the businesses that made them so rich in the first place. I associated Dorset with the wealthiest Wensley relatives. Whenever I went there, my socioeconomic discomfort level skyrocketed.

In addition, I had serious doubts about moving away from Bennington. Dorset felt isolated to me, far from my friends. If I moved in with Jill and Al, I'd have to give up Mount Anthony in my senior year and change to the Burr and Burton Seminary, an academically oriented private school, which was designated as the "public" high school for Dorset and Manchester.

It occurred to me that Al and Jill were geographically so inconvenient that maybe I should look for someone else to be my family. But each of my second thoughts would be followed by a frank discussion with them of my doubts and their fears, which would ultimately end with us knowing each other even better. My anxieties of having no friends in Dorset evaporated when a charming guy whom I had once met at a party called me and said he had heard I was moving to town. He asked me if I would like to go with him to the homecoming dance at the Burr and Burton Seminary and meet all the kids who would be in my class. I had a great time with all of them. Soon I got used to making the trek from the little house in Dorset down the pretty valley road to Manchester, where all the designer clothing people have their outlets and Al runs an Italian deli called Al Ducci's. Eventually I became totally hooked on Al's homemade mozzarella, basil, and tomato sandwiches. I found a gym there where I could work out on snowy weekends; I found two terrific ski mountains where I could go and play with my new friends.

Sometimes I'd walk outside the deli and catch the neighbors staring at me. I thought it was because they had seen my picture in the paper. But it turned out that they were staring because they remembered me—because Al's deli was right next door to the building where Duane and Diana and I had lived with Emma as little kids.

We'd go home to Dorset, and Al would tell fascinating stories about his grown children and the family cheese business, and Jill—who is the world's great animal lover—would tell stories about how she used to ride show horses when she was a kid and how each of her foster children had left her with a new cat. We'd end up sitting on the deck, all talked out, listening to music and eating chips.

Imperceptibly, over time, the question of leaving Bennington became a nonquestion. Many of my friends now had access to cars, so it was no trouble to get around. And the more I hung with Jill and absorbed her values, the more the idea of going to an academically oriented high school really appealed to me.

Of course, by then the question of "discipline" also now seemed sort of beside the point. My concerns about who would lock me up and who would let me out grew suddenly less hot, less vital, even irrelevant. It turned out that Jill was the one who set the curfews, who wanted to know where I was going and with whom—and when—I would be back. Al was much more philosophical. He had brought up three children, two boys and a girl. His theory was "Everybody has to learn what's right and wrong by themselves." Other than doing drugs or alcohol or any of that kind of stuff, he was pretty relaxed. "If Charlotte wants to go out and dance until two in the morning," he said, "that's her decision. And if she's exhausted the next day and oversleeps and misses her exam or her audition, that's her problem."

I felt together with these self-examined, thoughtful people. And accepted. And safe. The circle of trust that Valerie Miner sometimes spoke of was being drawn around me, as subtle and gentle and natural to my emotional environment as the green mountains surrounding Dorset.

The Last Crisis

WE HAD ONE major crisis right before I was supposed to move permanently from Bennington to Dorset. I had begun the some-times hectic process of preparing for the pageant in Biloxi, and I thought I might be just too lonely and isolated and inaccessible out in the quiet pine forests of Dorset.

But Jill and Al had prepared everything for my arrival. They had adjusted their business schedules and rearranged their home and their social obligations to make me welcome.

It came to a showdown.

Jill said that either I made my commitment and moved in with them for our six-month preadoption trial period as scheduled—or the process of adoption would stop.

I took a deep breath and said to myself, "Go for it, Charlotte." On July 12, I said goodbye to the house on Silver Street and all the people I had grown to love so much there, and I moved once more.

It may seem like nothing to be able to move into a lovely home with intelligent people at the age of sixteen. But for me, a foster kid, it was a huge achievement to be able to give up the temporary state that had characterized my whole life and that I was used to, to embrace the concept of permanence. I was used to sojourning. Settling down—as much as I wanted it—required a leap of faith for me. I think I got the presence of mind and the emotional calm that was necessary to do it from the understanding smile on Jill's face.

I began to think of Jill as my "friend-mother." Emma was my baby mother, Cari was my childhood mother, Janet was my teen mother, and Jill was going to be my friend forever.

It was a whole new idea.

It changed my life.

Pageant Shopping with
Lopez and Charles

FOR JILL AND me, shopping for clothes for the Biloxi pageant was an unbelievable challenge. Imagine looking for evening clothes for a beauty pageant with a woman who has never watched one all the way through and who wouldn't be caught dead in the kind of stuff you need to wear in them!

"Ball gowns," Jill will tell you with a wry grin, "are not my forte."

Still, if we were going to be in the same family with each other, we had to deal. The outfit for my interviews with the judges we found at the Anne Klein outlet: it was just perfect. But then we had to come up with *six* evening and cocktail dresses. Huge supplies of dressy clothes just don't exist where we live in Vermont. There was no choice but to go to Boston.

I had already made the bus trip from Manchester to Boston twice, because the Barbizon Modeling School office was there, and they handled all the pageant entrants from Maine, Vermont, New Hampshire, and Massachusetts. It's a terrible bus ride. A million stops. Long. Exhausting. And even though I'm athletic, I get tired. Jill thinks maybe I'm a little hypoglycemic, because I sometimes just sort of shut down and need a cup of cocoa or some Ben and Jerry's ice cream as a pick-me-up to restore my energy. She figured if I had to go alone on a one-day shopping marathon to Boston after a bus ride like that, I'd be wiped out. So she decided she would take the day off and we'd drive to Boston and go shopping together.

It was the sixth of July. Blazing hot. The air conditioning in the car wasn't working. I had received $3,000 for my pageant wardrobe, which seemed a gigantic amount of money to me. But Jill had a feeling in her heart that a lot of the girls in the pageant were very wealthy—somebody had told us that one of them was Barbara Mandrell's daughter—and she figured that for them, $3,000 would be just a drop in the bucket. The Barbizon staff saw that we were clueless as to where to shop in Boston, and they said well, okay, try here, try there. We went to a mall right nearby, and we went to two stores before we wound up in a place called Jessica McClintock.

I was trying on dresses in the back. We found one gown and we just loved it, and Jill went out to talk to the saleslady to see how much it was.

"Well, you realize it's seventy percent off," the saleslady said. "All the dresses on the plastic hangers are seventy percent off.

Whatever the price on the ticket is [and some them had been marked down already], take seventy percent off!"

Suddenly Jill was running back into the dressing room screaming, "Charlotte! Charlotte! Oh my God, Charlotte, listen to this." We realized that one dress was $30, one was $40. . . . It was incredible! We had been planning on spending $600 for two dresses. And suddenly I'm going, "The short pink or the long pink?" and Jill is going, "Take 'em both!" And I'm saying, "The green or the lavender?" and Jill is answering, "Hell, take 'em all!"

We wound up buying seven dresses—three long and four short—for $285! When we got back to Vermont and looked over our incredible haul, we felt thrilled. But Jill said she had a feeling in her heart that compared with the flounces and laces and ruffles and spangles that were probably going to show up in Mississippi, my main event evening dress wasn't quite dressy enough. So she asked the costume designer at the theater to take a look at it, and the costume designer went shopping and found some fabulous beaded trim. The night before I left for the pageant, Jill stayed up until two in the morning, sewing it on my dress. She said it was a way of paying back her own mother, because that was the kind of thing her mother would always do for her. That evening gown, the one I wore for the final round of the pageant in Biloxi, cost a total of $37.

Taking Janet

STILL, DESPITE THE success of our shopping trip, something was bothering me. I wanted *Janet* to come with me to Biloxi.

I wanted her to come because I had lived with her while I was going to the state pageant, and she had supported my getting involved in this thing in the first place. She had the biggest part in giving me the confidence to go for it. I had become a wise old soul at Janet's house. And strong. And people-smart. I had learned that bad things are really *supposed* to happen, just as much as good things, but that if you're strong—and you have faith—maybe you can make it through. Living with Janet finally made me aware of the *community* of foster children. Nobody in the country seemed to care that we were out there, almost half a million foster kids, and I felt that I now had something to say about the lives we were leading, something I wanted people to understand. The energy of that, the meaningfulness of it, came from Janet.

So when I was going to the national pageant, I wanted her to come along. And instead of being all uptight about my request and feeling challenged and insecure, Jill Charles and Al Scheps were totally cool about it and totally understood why I wanted it that way.

"Two weeks before the pageant in Biloxi," Janet recalls, "Charlotte moved in with Al and Jill. I had always wanted to go with her to the nationals, because it was our thing, the pageant stuff. But it wasn't my bailiwick anymore, and I figured she would be at the nationals with her new mom. Then one day, I got this call from Jill."

"Janet? What are you doing the week of August seventh?"

"I don't have any plans."

"Well, Charlotte would love you to go with her to Biloxi."

"Oh, that's very nice, Jill, but I sure don't know how I'm gonna get the money together in a week."

"Don't worry about that. Al and I and SRS put together the money for the plane. I'll make your reservations, and you go and have a wonderful time."

I don't think that either Janet or I will ever forget that phone call. It represented a kind of grace and generosity you don't see much in this mean old world.

A Nervous Goodbye

THE NEW ENGLAND contestants were supposed to meet up in the Boston area and then fly down to Biloxi together. That meant I had to spend the night before our departure at the home of a wonderful girl named January who was Miss Massachusetts Teen USA. Jill and Al and I got into the car with my two bags containing my seven bargain dresses and drove there. January's mother, Sandy, a vivacious, hospitable lady who's been putting January in these contests since she was a little girl, came running out to meet us, and the first thing she said was "Hi! Welcome! Where are your bags?"

I replied, "Right here. I have two bags—that's what we were told we could bring on the plane."

And Sandy said, "But January sent a hundred and fifty pounds of clothes down to Mississippi last week!"

Jill went into a panic. Her worst fears were coming true! I was indeed going to be the most underdressed girl at the Miss Teen USA Pageant. Sandy must have seen her face collapse, because she immediately tried to comfort us. "Oh, now, never mind," she said. "Don't worry about it. If Charlotte needs anything, she can borrow from January!"

In the house, there were dozens of pictures on the wall, of January winning all these awards—all over the kitchen and the rec room—pictures from when she was four and ten and fourteen, from when she had won the town pageant and the county pageant and then the state pageant. The pictures terrified Jill even more. She was ready to burst into tears. She was thinking,

My God! We're leaving this poor girl with these experienced pageant people in this crazy situation! She's just going to be destroyed!

But I—who usually had these conversations with myself—now laid one of my comfort trips on Jill. "No sweat," I said. "I can deal. All this might have made an impact on another girl, but not on me. I'm not going to feel inferior to other people just because they have more clothes. Come on, you know me better than that. If I can compete in a thirty-seven-dollar dress, it'll show everybody that it's not the dress but the person inside that counts. I'll keep a level head and do just fine."

And then Jill said something that turned out to be immeasurable comfort *for me*.

"Just keep your own personality, Charlotte. Don't let anybody change you. Don't think you have to behave a different way just because the other girls are different from you. Remember. Be yourself."

I hugged her. Al grinned at me. "Take it from me, kid," he said. "You got this baby sewed up, no contest, you're gonna win hands down. I got an instinct about these things."

They both hugged me again, and then they left.

I stayed overnight. January and her mother asked me all kinds of questions: what I would be wearing, what my life had been like in foster care, whether I was nervous. I kept saying "No," but we all knew what a crock that was. January's mother had a friend, Darlene, who was January's coach, a total expert about the pageant. We sat in the living room and watched a tape of the previous year's pageant. January had really studied that tape. They were so into it. I mean, I thought *I* was into it, but nothing like this! That night, Darlene was quizzing January with questions that the judges might ask. They asked me if I wanted to be quizzed too. I said, "No, that's okay." Because by now I too was having those "feelings in my heart" that Jill always got, and I thought that if I dared to rehearse, I might not come across as natural. I might not sound like me.

I was psyched.

As I went to sleep that night in January's house. I kept hearing Jill's voice:

Keep your own personality, Charlotte. Be yourself.

The Happy Journey to Victory

YOU HEAR TERRIBLE stuff about beauty pageants. Contestants stealing each other's shoes, insulting each other, making each other feel bad. But the girls I met in Biloxi were wonderful to each other. No backbiting, no nasty tricks. People complimented each other. Lent each other clothes. Told each other jokes. Invited you into their rooms to listen to tapes and hang out. It was like we knew we were all in it together. Sure, only one of us could win, but we knew for starters that we were all pretty terrific and very lucky, and that on the day after the pageant, no matter who had won, we would all still be pretty terrific and very lucky.

The most amazing thing was that I wasn't jealous!

Not jealous of January, or Miss Maine Teen USA, or Miss Florida Teen USA, or anybody! For the very first time in my life, I was with other people and I wasn't jealous of their families, their wealth, their opportunities, their educations, their clothes, their anything!

Maybe I had learned not to be jealous from Jill, who was totally gracious and cool about Janet being there with me in Biloxi and being interviewed by the press and saying she was my foster mother.

Maybe I had just lost my jealousy the minute I knew for sure that I would soon have a home and a family of my own. My

envy of other people and their families and their securities had
been like the chains and shackles that weighed down the really
bad, crazy kids who were brought in by the cops to Janet's
house. As long as I could remember, jealousy had weighed me
down, making my whole life heavy and bitter. And when I woke
up one morning in Mississippi and found that the awful seething
feeling was gone, I finally felt light and straight and strong and
really free.

PRELIMINARY NIGHT DIDN'T happen on TV. It was just presented for all the people out there in the audience. All of us girls
wore the same style of swimsuit. We could just feel the excitement of the people beyond the footlights. I loved being on stage.
In the spotlight. It gave me such a rush. I had always messed
with the idea of being an actress, but now I absolutely was *sure*.
I kept getting compliments that I was good on stage, that the
camera loved me. It gave me confidence.

But on the night of the telecast, when we knew millions of
people would soon be watching us, our gathering tension ex-
ploded, and we all became jittery as racehorses in the gate.

The manager said over the intercom: "Calm down, you're
going on in three minutes."

We all just screamed. It was so exciting, to imagine yourself
being seen all over the world, in thirty different countries.

"Two minutes. Okay, sixty seconds. Come on up, girls. Thirty
seconds."

It was wild—like a huge play-off game! I had a lot of confidence in myself. I was ready. I wasn't nervous being in a bathing
suit in front of all those people. I thought my knees would be
shaking, that I would be so sick with fear, but I wasn't. What
were those cameras anyway? Just metal boxes with little red

lights on top. I didn't think about the 30 million people. I just thought about the crowd that was there that night, the people I knew personally, like Janet, all decked out in her new scarlet dress (probably doing deep breathing to keep herself calm), and January's mother, Sandy; and the cops and the stage crew—the plain, regular people.

When we walked out in front of those cameras, the crowd went wild.

I cannot tell you how I loved that moment.

There was Dick Clark, the man who had so often starred in my dreams of stardom, in the flesh, grinning at us.

There was the orchestra, the drumroll, the lights I had imagined all my life.

I felt as if I was singing in the flower meadow again, standing on a tree stump and greeting my public in the mountains of Vermont. This night, this experience, this was all the sunshine in the world to me.

RIGHT AT THE very time when Dick Clark was greeting us on stage, a small crowd of people began gathering at the home of Jill and Al in Dorset. There was a show at the Dorset Theatre that night: *Relatively Speaking* by Alan Ayckbourne, a four-character play. Most likely, the actors were just like Jill and had never in their lives before paid much attention to a beauty contest. But Jill had been out with them earlier in the week, fascinating them with stories of the girls and their mothers and their clothes and their ambitions, and now they were all hooked. Of course, they had to go on stage on the night of the pageant and couldn't join Jill and Al at the house until after the curtain came down around ten o'clock. By that time, I had passed through the initial round of judging and had made it into the final twelve.

Nothing is taped in the Miss Teen USA Pageant. Everything happens right there on stage. So when you make it to the top twelve and you know you've actually got a shot at this thing, and your heart begins to race, and your stomach begins to churn, there's no place to hide, no way to yell "Cut!" or "Time out!" so you can go to the bathroom and collect yourself and fix your mascara. If you sweat and you laugh sort of hysterically and your hair falls apart, everybody sees. But you can't try to be in control at that point. You have to just be yourself and let the thing happen.

"THE ACTORS CAME running over from the theater as soon as they could," Jill recalled. "And then friends and neighbors started showing up. By the time Charlotte got into the final six, there were maybe a dozen people at the house. At every commercial the phone rang. It was like people all over Vermont were tuning in to this thing. My brother called from Brooklyn. My mother called from her home in the Catskills. Al's kids called from New Jersey. The lady from the bank in Dorset called me four times!

"After Dick Clark interviewed Charlotte, and she talked about foster care, and they flashed her score and *it was really high,* all these cool, sophisticated professional people began screaming and jumping up and down. Our poor cat Charity got so scared she hid behind the TV and became trapped in the wires and we had to rescue her. At the next commercial, an actor who had appeared in a play with our company earlier in the summer and had met Charlotte at that time called us from Atlanta, where he was doing another gig. He said he was in his motel room watching the pageant and becoming completely hysterical with excitement. The television cameras kept returning to Janet, who was wearing this scarlet dress, and her face was scarlet, too. I thought, *My God, poor Janet,* because she looked like she was going to have a stroke from the tension."

NOT ME. I was calm. I swear, I was absolutely calm. The hardest part about finding out that you're in the top six is that you know you are going to have to answer one question and you cannot imagine what it is going to be and your answer has a good chance of making or breaking your candidacy. While 30 million people watched, I was actually having one of my conversations with myself.

Do not be a jerk, Charlotte. Now is not the time to choke. People have asked you impossible questions every single day of your life—who do you love? what do you want? when are you coming home?—and you have always managed to answer them somehow. So tonight, just manage again, and come up with an answer.

They asked me what I would do if I could spend a day with Chelsea Clinton. It was certainly not the kind of question anybody could have rehearsed for. I answered as though I were having a casual conversation with a friend. Whatever I said just popped out of my mouth, and I had to make do with that.

IN THE MIDST of all the people in the house, Jill says she suddenly grew very calm. Very scholarly and statistical. While everyone else was whooping and hollering, she turned on her little calculator and began to fix on numbers and keeping score. Al Scheps, on the other hand, was bouncing up and down on the sofa, hollering "YESSSSS!" every time my scores flashed, as though he were back at a Giants game in the Meadowlands.

"It's all over! Charlotte's gonna win!" he exclaimed.

"Shhh, Al," said Jill, calculating. "Be quiet."

"She's a shoo-in!"

"Please. Look at the runners-up, for God's sakes! Miss Pennsylvania! Miss Indiana! These are gorgeous, well-spoken girls."

"Break out the bubbly! I got an instinct for these things! The kid's got the pageant in the bag!"

"Al! Please! Let's not get our hopes up."

And then I won.

I LEARNED THAT I was the winner exactly when the audience did. Right there. On stage.

After all my calm, my cool, my years of interior conversations, I just lost it.

In my mind's ear, I could just hear the roar of victory at home that rose up from the misty mountains, over the lakes and the pines. The actors who were there say it's true, that's exactly what happened.

I did not do an elegant job of representing my fellow Vermonters at that moment. I was sweating and crying and my hair flew all over, and somebody put a crown on my head and flowers in my arms, and all the other girls were mobbing me and kissing and hugging me, and the crown fell off, and I thought I would faint from happiness.

Then I had to do an interview. All the lights, the bright colors, the audience, the cameras, the judges, celebrities—it was all so paralyzing. I was smiling and smiling and smiling. I was truly happy, but I suddenly felt really wiped out. My feet were starting to hurt in my high heels. I had to march all the way through the ballroom, make a speech, greet people, kiss everybody. A huge party was going on, and people constantly hugged me and kissed me. People touching me. Picture. Picture. Autograph. I felt like a quarterback being sacked. I was not used to it. I just wanted to sit down. And I had to keep smiling, because everyone was taking my picture.

The cheering crowds gave me my second wind. So I danced and laughed and tried to keep the crown from falling off and gave my roses to Janet, who was simply apoplectic with joy, and I tried not to say anything too silly to the reporters.

Then I got tired again.

Exhausted.

My voice just disappeared.

I actually thought about not calling anybody at home. But then I thought, *No, Charlotte, you've got to.* I knew that all over Vermont, people were exulting for me, for us. In my heart I could hear them cheering. *You've got to call, Charlotte,* I said to myself. *These are the people who care about you.*

Diana was the first person I called. She wasn't there. Cari answered. She was crying with happiness. Bill got on the other line. He was crying, too. I realized that despite our differences, these foster parents cared deeply about me and had contributed enormously to making me the person I had become.

Diana had gone to someone's house to watch the pageant with a bunch of friends, and when I won, they all went crazy and Diana ran outside screaming, and the cops came with sirens, because they thought maybe she had been attacked or something.

I called Dan. He was out pacing in the driveway, waiting for me to call. His family was in an uproar. People we knew were driving by and honking—the Shit Kickers and Harriet and Vera, Lucy and Peaches and the track team, and the whole gang from Janet's house—all honking and howling down Main Street in Bennington like after a football game when you win the championship. I guess the pageant was a kind of championship for our town.

Then I called Jill.

All her company had finally gone home. She and Al were in bed. I could just see them cuddling up to each other with the phone between them.

"What'd I tell you?" Al roared. "Didn't I tell you? I told you you'd win hands down. I got an instinct about these things."

Jill got on the phone.

"You were wonderful. You were perfect. Congratulations. Don't sign anything until I get there. I'll be there tomorrow."

"I'm starving," I said.

"Order an ice cream."

"They ordered me a pizza, but I'm too excited to eat."

She laughed. And then there was this breath of silence between us.

"I'm so proud of you, Charlotte. I love you so much."

"I love you too, Jill."

I thought it was the moment of my greatest victory.

But it wasn't.

That came some months later, on March 7, 1994, when Jill and Al adopted me and became my parents.

EPILOGUE

I COULD WRITE a whole second book about what happened to me during the year that I was Miss Teen USA. With the wonderful Miss Universe people guiding me and shepherding me (and the wonderful teachers at Burr and Burton helping me catch up on my studies when I occasionally came home), I crisscrossed the country again and again and spoke to literally thousands of foster kids and their parents and the social workers and legal and police personnel who are involved with them. Sometimes I thought I was dreaming. All these MSWs and PhDs and CHINs and Esqs sitting out there in the audience, their faces lifted in my direction, waiting for *me* to give them advice! I actually testified before legislators! Once I was even on the same platform with U.S. Attorney General Janet Reno!

Not all of this attention has been absolutely delightful, let me tell you. The media can get a little overzealous sometimes. After I won the pageant, a camera crew arrived in Vermont and started knocking on my friends' doors and interviewing them and shooting footage of them. Some of the kids themselves thought that was terrific, but me, I hated it. I felt I was entitled to my private life and couldn't wait for these people to leave us alone.

Then *Inside Edition* decided to do a story on me. Great, right? Not right. What they didn't tell me was that they were going to beat the bushes and find my mother. I was in Florida with Diana, doing *Star Search* with Ed McMahon. I turned on the TV and *surprise!* there she was: Emma Lopez Caraballo. You can bet I was pretty upset. Because I remembered my mother, and this was not how I had imagined seeing her for the first time in eleven years! (Diana didn't remember her and felt totally undisturbed by seeing her on TV. "Gee," she said, "now I know where I got my nose from." I'll say it again: that one-year difference in our ages—what an enormous difference it made in us.)

My goal in making all these appearances was to become a national advocate for foster children, to wake up the country to their existence and their problems. I was sick of the attitude that some people had toward foster children: that they were bad kids who had wound up in foster care because they had done something wrong. I knew that wasn't true. Most kids are in foster care because of reasons beyond their control. Someone needed to say that, to stick up for the kids. Winning the pageant made me that spokesperson.

In the many discussions that I had with these audiences across the country, certain issues came up repeatedly, which means they must be very important.

People who have foster kids or who are attempting to adopt a child must always try to remember where those children have just come from.

Now that I am studying acting, I have learned that it is extremely important to reconstruct the moment before a scene, so that you have an idea where your character is coming from emotionally and environmentally. The same advice should be given to people who are taking in foster kids. Remember where they just were. Try to simulate for yourself what they have been through and how it has affected them. If a child has come into your home because his parents have abused him, it probably isn't very wise to use spanking as a punishment, for example. It's much easier to handle a child with odd characteristics and personality traits if you know his history. Many may appear to be angry. Don't take it personally. Many may ask for a lot of attention. Don't reject them. They may want to be held and told that they're not going to be taken away. Soothe them, but don't give them false hopes if it is not your intention to keep them.

If you have to be moved out of a home when you're a little kid, you must be told repeatedly and emphatically that it is not your fault that you are being moved, that the people in the home think you're wonderful, that something else has come up which makes it impossible for you to stay there.

If you are allowed to blame yourself for your foster-ness as a little kid, it will create a legacy of self-doubt and insecurity that will haunt you your whole life.

When Diana and I were moved in and out of homes as little children, we got no explanation, no reassurance. It was just "We're going for a ride, girls," and off we would go, never to come back.

Of course, I blamed myself for these sudden dislocations.

Kids always blame themselves.

Only grown-ups are complicated enough to blame other people. I always felt that I had done something wrong or that I had some kind of disease. The insecurity from that has haunted me ever since.

Kids have to be educated about the situation they're in, so they're not confused when they are little. If no one tells them it's not their fault, then they grow up feeling like losers. If the social workers have to exaggerate, to bend over backward to make this point, then so be it. The basic requirement for being able to

grow up successfully despite your foster-ness is a clear con-
science.

*When potential foster parents take training courses like the
one that Valerie Miner gives in Vermont, they should be told
they have one great gift to give: UNEQUIVOCAL EMO-
TIONAL SUPPORT.*

You cannot believe in yourself unless your foster family be-
lieves in you, unless they say, "Keep up the good work; do what
works for you."

I got a lot of support from my various foster parents, and it
helped me enormously. But a lot of my time in foster care, I also
felt very alone. Many of the kids I talked to say they feel too shy
to ask for more than the bare essentials. They've been taught to
be so grateful for the food and the board and the lifts to school
that they're ashamed to say they need moral support, too. But
they do. Even if kids are with you for only a week, you've got
to let them know that you are there for them, that you believe
in them. Among the rules and the regulations and the curfews
and the reports, an encouraging word, a compliment, a simple
"You can do it" makes all the difference in the world, because
the biggest part of getting ahead is having people believe in you.

I think the reason my relationship with the Wensleys shattered
was that it was always equivocal; there were always all sorts of
nicks and cracks that ultimately made everything fall apart.
With all the battling and confusion between them and SRS that
I've read about in the case files, it is obvious to me that they
were very uncertain about adoption. Of course, the grown-ups
did a good job of hiding all of these technical difficulties. But
even if I didn't know the facts, I knew something was wrong.
The way they felt was always apparent to me. So much doubt
and distance lay between us that I never really believed they

would be parents who would always be there for me and love me unconditionally. As a result, it was all too easy for me to leave.

Sibling reunification really helps to strengthen kids and make them confident enough to survive in the system.

I know that foster parents sometimes feel challenged by the presence of a natural or part-natural brother or sister—that they don't want to have kids around who "represent" the old family. Carol Wehner, Duane's foster mother, said that she was adopted herself, and her adoptive mother was just crazed by the idea that she and her sister might meet up with relatives from the natural family. I also realize that when siblings are placed in separate foster homes, it may be tough for their foster parents to socialize regularly when they may not particularly enjoy each other's company. And that the kids themselves may not wish to see their brothers and sisters, especially if it triggers bad memories.

But I tell you, the absence of a blood connection is like a hole in your soul. To be all nurture and no nature is to be like an artificial person. If I hadn't had Diana, I think I would have gone nuts. The idea that Duane lived so close to us all those years and we still never saw him—that really gets me crazy. And now that I've heard that Emma had at least three more children by other men and that those kids are out there somewhere— half brothers and sisters to the three of us—it electrifies me with curiosity and longing.

In the end, Duane, Diana, and I each ended up with a different family. But at least we *know* each other. At least we *see* each other. I realize that separation is the only alternative sometimes. There are very few foster families that can take in two or three kids. But I do think that in the end, it helps foster parents to keep their kids in touch with siblings, because the knowledge of a natural family creates confidence and calm.

There is very often not enough direct, positive communication between foster kids and the social workers who are making the decisions that influence their lives.

Many foster kids don't see their social workers that often. The workers are often too busy dishing *about* you with your foster parents to talk *with* you about anything. The system pushes social workers to hang with other grown-ups, because it seems to assume that grown-ups are more reliable reporters than kids are. I'm not at all convinced that that's true.

If my voice had been heard directly in my case files when I was seven and nine and thirteen, those files might have told a much richer and more complicated story. For years, nobody reported to my case files what I had to say, and as a result, the so-called record of my life is really largely a record of what my caretakers thought. They cannot possibly tell the whole story. *Kids need to be heard!*

Lots of kids say they are sure their social workers don't like them. This may be insecurity speaking, but the truth is, once you have that impression, you feel that you have an "enemy in court," and it makes you frightened and cagy and inclined to throw up your hands and say, "Up the system."

When I was blowing out of the Wensleys' house at fourteen, I was completely convinced that my adoption worker didn't like me. That impression was modified when I read my case files— but I didn't get to read them until long after the psychic damage was done.

If I had had more communication with this person and the other social workers who were handling my case at the time, I would have felt less alone, less desperate. Maybe one of these people could have interpreted my moods to my foster parents, or explained their rigidity to me—somehow helped us to talk to each other. If I had been able to really talk to my caseworkers about what was eating me, about how brokenhearted I felt about not being adopted, how frustrated I felt with the limitations of my life, maybe the system wouldn't have let me sit there in extended foster care for so long.

Catherine Cadieux has explained that social workers in Vermont had to drive huge distances to reach their cases. And I understand from her that when the workers left our house, they were probably heading over the mountains and through the valleys to some other kid, and after that, they most likely faced a gigantic pile of paperwork back at the office. But I also know that the Vermont system is probably one of the *least* overburdened in the country. According to Commissioner Young, in the country as a whole between 1985 and 1990, the number of kids in custody rose by 47 percent. In Vermont, it rose only 7 percent, largely because the state has been so successful in reuniting natural families. There are about 1,200 kids in paid placement in the whole state of Vermont now. So if there wasn't enough time to talk things through in Shaftsbury, imagine what it's like in some huge megalopolis like New York or Los Angeles!

We need more workers who can spend more time with fewer kids.

In my experience, a wise, loving older person who has some time and some resources can make all the difference in the life of a foster child.

I know that there are probably a gazillion people out there like Grammy, people who have worked hard all their lives and who have some leisure now and maybe a car, who can take the time to pay attention to a needful foster child. Organizations like Foster Grandparents should be replicated all over, in a

Grammy Corps that would pick up the slack for the social workers and serve as backup for the system. They could do all the things the system hasn't got time to do. Talk. Listen. Care. Wait. Encourage. Reward. And I'll bet in the course of conversation, they could figure out a few things that the kids could do to help them, too.

Kids give up in the foster care system. It rewards them with attention for bad behavior; but for good behavior, it rewards them with exactly zippo.

There's no incentive to achieve, nothing to fire up their enthusiasm. So the enthusiasm gets beaten out of them, and a lot of foster kids become whiny and angry and selfish. So many kids are so frustrated by the bad things that have happened to them that they take out their frustrations on everybody around them. They don't care about *themselves,* never mind their social workers or their foster parents. Look at how badly some of the kids in Janet's house treated her! Look at how badly they treated themselves!

When kids enter foster care, they are made to assume a position of helpless dependency—and they know it. It's a lose-lose situation. People treat you as if *you owe the state* for taking care of you. So in self-defense, you begin to act as if *the state owes you* a way out of your situation.

A lot of kids I met on the road after I won the pageant had gotten so they really just make a career out of feeling sorry for themselves. They don't do anything with their lives. They just sit around waiting for something to happen to them.

So nothing happens.

And no one helps.

Who wants to help someone who is bitter and expects everybody else to fix their problems?

I believe the only way to break out of this awful mess of negative attitudes is to give foster children incentives to improve their lives. Janet Henry intuitively understood and implemented this concept in giving happy faces, financial incentives for making good grades, and time-out incentives for helping with the housework. Maybe somebody can figure out how to apply this principle on a broader scale.

Poverty goes hand in hand with being a foster child. That's a big problem. For everybody.

When you are young, foster care payments simply do not support the kinds of activities you need to be involved in to break the cycle of emotional dependency. Activities—like school teams, student government, choral groups, dance classes, clubs, and camps—are all membership-related and give you confidence and a sense of belonging, but they also usually cost money. If all your money is going to put sneakers on your feet, how can you join anything? There needs to be a redefinition of what "special needs" are and a realization that one of the biggest handicaps for a foster child is isolation. You just can't grow alone. You can't become a citizen on the fringe of the community.

In another example of the official poverty of foster children, a kid who lives in the system and then ages out of it often never directly sees any of the money that the state has laid out on her behalf. In most cases, nothing has been saved for the crucial years after eighteen, when you're on your own for the first time. So a college education turns out to be a wild dream for most of us.

I'd like to see somebody figure out a system in which a kid who is doing well in school and who is clearly college material would have a college fund set aside from her foster care money so that when she left the system, there would be some college tuition already in the till.

Foster kids need each other. In the absence of settled homes, in the absence of brothers and sisters, they can be a tremendous support for each other if only their social workers can wrestle them into each other's company.

When I went into the group home and met all those other foster kids, I actually learned to feel better about myself and gained self-confidence, because I knew I was not the only one going through these tough times. Foster kids in a local area should have regular meetings with each other, not for therapy or anything complicated, but just for fun—brotherhood and sisterhood.

Maybe there's just a little too much emphasis these days on the rights of natural parents.

I think parents should have to prove themselves. If a man leaves a woman pregnant and never pays any attention to his child until one day—when he realizes that the child has been adopted by somebody he doesn't like—he should not be able to march in and claim paternity and get that child back. Particularly if that child is in a happy, safe, loving home.

The same thing goes for the children of drug addicts. I read in the paper about a little girl who was taken away from her drug-addicted mother and given to foster parents who loved her and raised her and made her healthy. When she was almost three years old, her mother was pronounced cured by the drug authorities. And up she came to the front door of this foster home, with a teddy bear and a healthy body, saying, "Thanks a lot for keeping my baby, folks. Now I want her back."

It's a great day for the cured drug addict.

But what about the poor little girl?

She's being torn out of the arms of her devastated foster parents to be reunited with this stranger, and you can bet your life she is going to blame herself. The system shouldn't toy with the emotions of children that way.

If a parent is a drug addict and can't take care of her child, she should be forced to give up the child. If she gets well enough to take care of a child again and she wants to be a mother, fine. Then she should take care of some other drug addict's baby, the same way that a good-hearted stranger took care of her baby.

I know it sounds cruel. But it's only cruel for the mother, and she'll survive. For the kid, it's the kindest way.

A foster child should be able to see the case files whenever he or she is mature and ready and willing to see them.

I didn't see mine until I was seventeen years old. That was much too late. There you are, a ward of the state, engulfed by self-doubt, and the book of your life is under lock and key in some vault. I was very angry about that, and let me tell you, the kids that I have spoken to out there are angry, too. We all want to know what our past was about, why we weren't with Mom and Dad and who they were and what they were like. We all want to know why this or that decision was taken in our behalf.

When you are old enough to want to see your files, then that's when you should see them.

EVERYONE WANTS TO be loved. Love is harder to come by for some than others. We foster kids didn't choose to be born into this world to be rejected or abused by our own biological parents. But if we are the unlucky ones, then we have to move on. We can't do that—especially as children—if we don't have people in our lives who are willing to make a full commitment to us and our situation with the unconditional love and support that any parents would give to their own child. There has to be respect and devotion from both sides to make a lasting relationship.

In the end, I believe that being in foster care made me a stronger person. No one will take advantage of me. No one will manipulate me. But I know that I could not have survived all this without the help and the company of God. I give everything I have to God. I don't have to go to church every minute and get down on my knees and pray in front of everybody. I can just sit in a chair and speak to God like a friend, and I know He is with me. When other foster kids ask me how I got so far, I say it was because the Lord was always walking beside me, giving me guidance and comfort. He brought through a miracle. If He hadn't, I would never have made it.

Sometimes, when I'm making a speech and the lights are on me and everybody is waiting to hear what I have to say, I get scared. What I am I doing there?

But then I have a sense that there's this circle of people around the room and the audience and me—all the many social workers from SRS who did their best to keep me safe and secure, all the foster parents who took such good care of me, my brother Duane and my sister Diana and all the sisters and brothers I have had along the way, my friends who introduced me to the wide world, and the pageant people who brought a treasure of happiness and security within reach—all of these people are sort of holding hands in my vision and dancing slowly around me.

For me, this is the "circle of trust" that Valerie Miner spoke about.

It was completed by Al and Jill the day they adopted me and made me their daughter. When I think of myself inside this circle, I know I'm safe, I know I'm loved, and I don't feel scared anymore.

That's the circle that must be drawn around every foster child.

I know I am living proof that no matter who you are or what

circumstances you are in, you can do whatever you want with your life *if only you believe in yourself!* Everybody goes through upheavals as a teenager. I've tried to be absolutely honest about mine, so that foster kids going through the torments of insecurity in adolescence will know that they are perfectly normal and not alone. I realize how lucky I have been, and I want so much to inspire other foster kids to imagine that they can make their lives come out okay as I did. I want to give those kids hope that they can not just endure their situation but succeed in spite of it; that foster-ness doesn't necessarily have to be a one-way ticket to self-doubt and failure; that with will and determination, they can seize control of their own lives, notice opportunity when it shows up, make their own good fortune, and ultimately beat the system.